This book is dedicated to:
All survivors of suicide; the loved one's left behind,
to those who've attempted,
and one's who've thought about it.

For everyone who is an organ donor and to all recipients
living on through them; ensuring you see your loved
one live on in another life. Recipients, please do not feel
guilty that you are alive and your donor is not. They
chose to be donors, so live your 2nd chance
at life to the fullest!

To My Husband:
You are my rock and I couldn't have survived
without your love and support! Thank you for cheering
me on in my goals of becoming an advocate in hopes of
helping end this epidemic!

To My Daughter:
You've had a successful first year of college and
we couldn't be more proud of you! We know
great things are in store for your future!

To Our Family & Friends:
Thank you all for your support of my first book
and for loving us, supporting us, and
continually praying for us as we learn to survive living
without Pierce after our year of first.

some names have been changed

Forward:

I have known Bobbi for over 30 years. This should not have happened to her or her family; nor, should suicide happen to any family or anyone.

Bobbi has poured her heart and soul into this 2nd book; as she did the first one, "Our Year of First Without You" 'A journey through suicide and organ donation'. Her desire to shed light on suicide through her personal loss is evident in her passion to save others from this pain!

I recently told a client that the one thing I wanted was him not to feel guilty about his son's suicide. He said, "Easier said than done". My only answer was BLAME DEPRESSION, not him or yourself.

Those who want out of this unbearable pain can think of nothing else but to escape. They are Masters of Deception and they go to great lengths to conceal their plan. Bobbi explicitly points this growing problem throughout this book.

If you have ever experienced this 'black hole', you understand. If you haven't, please don't judge.

Her wish is to help others. May her book reach those who are in need.
God bless Bobbi for sharing her story.

-Loretta Bruce M.S., L.P.C.

Intro:

So much has happened in our lives since my first book
"Our Year of First Without You" 'A journey through
suicide and organ donation' that I felt compelled to write
this book to continue to share our story with you.

Surviving the death of any loved one is difficult.
It is far worse when your loved one dies from depression;
thus, taking their own life. The guilt associated with the
death is compounded by the question of why: why couldn't
I save them, why wasn't I enough for them to want to live,
why didn't our efforts to help them work? This is all
compounded by the what should have beens and
the what will never be.

The fracture it leaves upon a family has lingering effects
for years to come; I'm sure it must, as we are just two years
into our loss.

The child(ren) left behind are dealing with their own pain,
seeing their parents pain, and needing their parents to be
there for them. They so want them to be okay; yet this is
compounded by their feelings that it's now all about the
one who died; yet, 'hey, look at me! I'm still here.'

They, not being parents, can't imagine our hurt and feeling
of being lost. They can't comprehend why we will *never
not say* their name. We will never forget our child and
never stop missing him; but, we are healing and moving
forward. He doesn't occupy every single moment, of every
single day, just as he didn't when he was alive. We find
reasons to smile, to celebrate, to have fun and live again;
yet, it catches back up to us and we take a small step back;
knowing, we'll be okay, we'll regain our footing.

For the parents, not ever experiencing something like this; the loss of a child is horrific, but far worse when it's suicide.

Those parents continually wonder: what more could I have done? Did I say the wrong thing, or not say the right thing? Did I miss something? Then the guilt; especially in our situation, of Pierce with the girlfriend. We should have stepped in sooner and put our foot down on how much time was being spent together. When it became toxic, we should have ended it for him; but, teens are sneaky and have a way of doing things you're unaware of, unfortunately.

August 2016

Today's milestone is a mixed bag of emotions. While I'm thrilled & happy for Morgan to take this next step in her life, I'm saddened that P should be doing so as well; yet, he's robbed of this moment. My heart is literally torn in two. The unjust of it all is compounded by Morgan running into Sarah* (P's ex) last night & that she had the audacity to actually wave & smile at her!!!???!! Can we please just not have them invade our lives anymore? Is that seriously too much to ask?!?! Thankfully Morgan is now in a new town, far away from them & won't have to see them again!!! Morgan moved to Stephenville to start college. She is attending the junior college there with plans to transfer to a university next year.

My crazy, unexpected thoughts of emptiness........

1) odd/empty feel to the house
2) calmness in the house
3) not wondering if/when they're coming home (Yike's, scratch that, wondering when SHE is coming home.)
4) house still as clean as ya left it
5) why did I get a puppy to blow all this peace! (JK - we luv our LaDeaux!)

The following weekend, Shani and I attended our 30th high school reunion. I was hesitant to go at first; because while I wanted to see fellow classmates, I didn't want the 'pitty-party' and discussions of Pierce. I just wanted to attend, catch up with ole friends and enjoy myself. So, I went on the reunion page and posted 'that while many know about the loss of our son and I appreciate all the thoughts and prayers, I am attending to catch up and have fun, so I respectfully request we not discuss our situation.'

Uber ride to reunion

After the reunion, I had previously bought us tickets to see Stony LaRue at Billy Bobs. I bawled hysterically as he played 'Velvet'. We stayed the night at the Stockyards Hotel and had a great brunch Sunday morning.

Fall 2016

Morgan is having a terrific first semester and was invited to join the Phi Theta Kappa Honor Society! We couldn't be more proud of her! She is planning on double majoring in Dietetics and Sports Medicine. Her dream job after college is to work for a sports team or a University designing the meal plans for athletes. She is also into body building and spends a lot of time at the gym and cooking/meal prepping.

Tim has returned to running and managing his businesses. It takes time after losing someone; especially to suicide, to regain your life.

After a loss of this magnitude, you really start to examine your life; before, during, and after, to evaluate what changes need to be made and set forward a plan to implement those changes.

My first book was finally completed and ordered. It arrived in September and the majority of my time was spent promoting it, donating it to local high schools, and launching my website www.SurvivingOurSonsSuicide.com.

My major in college was advertising with a minor in marketing; thus, I am capable of promoting my book. I was interviewed by a local TV station after they received my Press Release. Several articles have been written about my book and my advocacy; thus far, I sold/donated over 500 books in the first 6 months!

My and Morgan's relationship is very strained at this point. When she comes home to visit from college over the weekend, we usually end up in a fight. She does not want to deal with losing her brother; thus, she does not want his name mentioned around her.

I asked my therapist about this and she said it's very common when siblings lose a sibling. They usually won't deal with the death until about the 2 -3 year mark. She also said that Morgan 'just needs Pierce to be dead', not to hear from us about the signs we get from him.

Morgan's roommate commented to me how OCD she is. It's to the point that if her she does the dishes, Morgan comes home, takes them out of the dishwasher, scrubs them down and re-loads it. She has NEVER been OCD in her life! It was Pierce who was OCD. My therapist said this is because emotionally, inside, everything is out of control; but, by doing this, she can control her environment.

My books arrived mid-September!!!! I held a book signing event at our home for friends and family. It's surreal to see all your hard work finally completed!

Surviving our son's suicide

'Our Year of First Without You'

A JOURNEY THROUGH SUICIDE AND ORGAN DONATION

Bobbi Gilbert

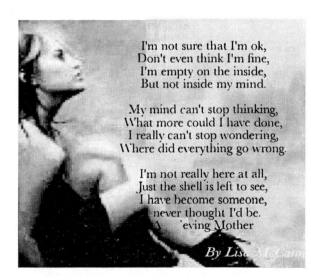

I'm not sure that I'm ok,
Don't even think I'm fine,
I'm empty on the inside,
But not inside my mind.

My mind can't stop thinking,
What more could I have done,
I really can't stop wondering,
Where did everything go wrong.

I'm not really here at all,
Just the shell is left to see,
I have become someone,
never thought I'd be.
'eving Mother

By Lisa McCann

Pierce's kidney/pancreas, Alicia, got engaged! We are so excited for Alicia and Brad! Can't wait until the big day arrives in May!

On the 11th, we had a major scare! Bryant, Pierce's lung recipient, was being transferred by ambulance from Lubbock to UT Southwestern in Dallas. We weren't sure what was going on, but were fearful he was rejecting. After speaking to his mom, I told her I'd meet her there. Her mother also came to be with them.

We sat in the waiting room most of the afternoon, visiting while the doctor's worked to figure out what was going on with Bryant. Later in the afternoon, his mom went back to his room. His grandmother asked me, "What are you even doing here?" I said, "Oh my, I'm so sorry if I've over stretched my bounds or if I've stayed too long," as I got up to leave. She said, "No, that's not what I mean. I'm asking, how, after everything you've been through, how can you even be here – in a hospital?" I explained that it was Bryant, a part of Pierce, so I had to be here.

Thankfully, the doctors were able to figure out what was going on with Bryant. He was having a reaction to having surgery. While there is no cure, it's treatable with two medications. When I got home that night, I broke down crying. The thought of losing one of his recipients is just too much for me to handle. I can't bear the thought of losing a part of him again.

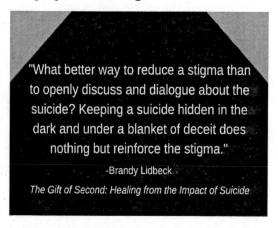

"What better way to reduce a stigma than to openly discuss and dialogue about the suicide? Keeping a suicide hidden in the dark and under a blanket of deceit does nothing but reinforce the stigma."

-Brandy Lidbeck

The Gift of Second: Healing from the Impact of Suicide

On the 29th, we attended the annual gala at the Italian Club of Dallas with our friends the Strippolli's. It was a fun evening with fantastic food and dancing! We have attended this event with them the past several years. The highlights are a silent auction and a multi-course Italian meal paired with wines. It is always a fun, festive event!

My post from Oct. 31st:

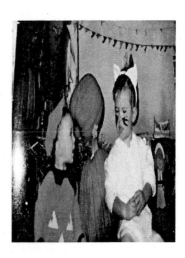

'When all has been forgotten,
still our song lives on.'
- from the movie 'Beauty and the Beast.

November 2016:

I was adopted as an infant and never wanted to know anything about my birth family; due to, I was blessed being raised by an incredible family. I never felt any different than my brothers, who are my parent's bio-logical kids.

When I turned 40, I decided I was ready to find my bio-logical family, mainly for medical records. I found my bio-logical uncle in Louisiana and he's been wonderful to me; providing me with, info, photo's, etc. He spoke to his sister Jan, who is my bio-logical mom, to let her know I found them. She said, "I can have nothing to do with her because my husband of 25 years knows nothing about her and he'll would wonder what else I've lied about."

Danny informed me she had a son, two years after having me; who also, knows nothing about me. He was raised as an only child, with his time split between her and their parents. He stated, 'You're the lucky one since she didn't raise you", stating how different my life would be if she did.

When I originally contacted Danny, I explained it was not my intent to cause harm or disrupt anyone's life. I kept my word for 8 years; but, since Pierce's passing, things have changed. I think her son, my half-brother, has a right to know about me. So, I called Danny to get his name, recalling that he lived in Chicago. He asked why and when I told him, he said he wanted nothing to do with this. No worries, the internet is an amazing thing and I located him in 15 minutes.

The following day, election day, I met my mom and aunt to celebrate my mom's birthday and my book. On the way, I dropped a copy of the book in the mail for Josh. On the outside of the book, I put a post-it-note with the following written on it:
Josh, if you will open this book and read the dedication on the first page, you will understand why you have received it.

On the inside, I wrote: 'Although we've never met, we have a lot in common. News flash: you're not an only child. You have a half-sister in Texas. Mommie Dearest knows about me and wants nothing to do with me; but it's okay because, Uncle Danny has been great to me, providing me info, medical records and photos.'

I received a text from Jan that afternoon (since Danny, who didn't want to be involved, told her what I was going to do), begging me not to send the book or contact Josh since he knows nothing about me and it would be hurtful to him and oh, sorry for your loss.

I was livid!!! HOW DARE SHE ask a favor of me when she couldn't be bothered to meet me or my kids after all these years; yet now, now that her lies are going to be exposed, she has the nerve to contact me! My reply was 'too late Mommie Dearest, I already mailed the book. One might suggest you get ahead of this and tell Josh about me before he gets the book.' (of course, she didn't!)

Two days later, I received an e-mail from Josh, saying: how glad he was that I reached out to him, how sorry they are for our loss of Pierce, and that he can't wait to get to know me better, that he always wanted a sibling. We texted daily for over a week and finally spoke on the phone a week later. He told me he had applied for a job in Ft. Worth the week before he received the copy of the book!

After we talked on the phone, Pierce told Tim he wished he could have met Josh. We made plans for his family to visit after Christmas. He and I are a lot alike in that we have a similar sense of humor. Morgan laughed about us continually picking on each other when we talk on the phone. She said, "Y'all act like 12 year olds!" Well, we've gotta start somewhere since there's lots of lost time to make up for.

We'll yeah, cuz only the 'Patriot's' chiro lets in us little people⊠
Dr. ⊠oe Ford w⊠Vitality Sports Medicine

Prayer warriors....URGENT! Our banker's daughter, Charity, who was serving in the Navy, 32 years old, mother of 2, took her own life Monday. There's only so much one woman can take! Pray Lora finds her way through this & can survive it to be here for her grandchildren!

So this just happened!!!!! Interviewed today by KXII about my book!!! It will air tomorrow either @6 or 10!! #weregounviralbaby#Jesustakethewheel#TeamPierce

God keeps putting angels in our path...today it's Jeff Askey. He owns Asky body shop in Decatur. He's repairing P's stang after David Ray hit a deer in it, heading home from the book signing party. The adjuster came out & had it in the $8k in damage & was going to total it. Jeff would have NONE of that knowing the history!!! So he took his time out of it & is searching DFW for after- market parts!!!

Several post from middle of the month:

All, for Christmas, do me a favor and consider buying a couple of books to donate to your local high school libraries. They may be purchased on my site or Amazon. For larger districts, you will have to obtain the superintendents permission. For smaller districts, you can simply walk into the HS office and donate it. HO-HO-HO! & Mucho Gracias!

One of my high school friends ordered several copies. She approached Aledo HS and was told the only self-help books they accept are one's about bullying. WTH??!! Last time I checked, bullying often leads to suicide. Ft. Worth ISD told her all self-help books are kept under lock and key and the librarian discerns who needs them. Again, WTH??!! As if a kid is going to say to the librarian, 'Hey, I'm suicidal, got a book that can help?'

A local Texoma school said no because 'it's not appropriate for children.' Ok!!?? It's not like I'm trying to donate to elementary schools, or even middle (although I think they should be in middle schools); so the question is, 'just exactly what are your high school students allowed to read? Dr. Suess? If they can read about the Holocausst and Civil Wars, why not suicide?

Why is it, MADD is allowed to stage horrific, re-enactments of a drunk driving wreck right before prom, but SHHHH! Don't ya dare say suicide!! If we don't talk about it, how are we: going to remover the stigma attached to it; going to let our kids know they way they are feeling is normal and you're not alone & you can ask for help!

One of P's friends, who struggled with depression after his passing, was thrilled my mission is to donate it to high schools. When he looked for something on the subject, it was all medical jargon. He feels my book will be way more appealing to teens since it's a true story and relatable.

GREATNESS!!! When ya finally connect w/ a half sibling, ya never knew cuz ya were adopted & he's all happy to know about ya, in text ex-change, the deplorable"makes the mistake of sayin', "you're livin' the life kid!" While I appreciate the props...ummmm, NOOOO!!!!! For once in my life, I'm not the baby in the family; so suck it up butter cup, you're about to endure 48 years of repressed come-uppins!!!!

WHITEWRIGHT, Texas (KXII) -- **A local mother is shining light on suicide. She wrote a book to honor her son who took his own life in April 2015.**
"Pierce was fiery, stubborn, brilliant, funny, charming - arrogant - loving, caring and giving," Bobbi Gilbert, Pierce's mom said smiling. Gilbert recalls the heart-breaking moment an officer showed up at her door around 6 a.m. to tell her that her 17-year-old old son committed suicide.
"He said, 'Ma'am, the Collin County sheriff asked me to contact you,' and that's when I knew. That's when I knew my world of first started without you," said Gilbert.
'Our Year of First Without You,' the title of the book Gilbert wrote about her journey through suicide and organ donation. "The beginning was really hard because it was going back there again and going back to what we had already passed and survived," said Gilbert. "But once I got to the part of meeting the recipients and the light, that's where the goodness came out and you got to see Pierce." Pierce was an organ donor and saved five lives with six of his organs. "When I was 11 years old, I had Leukemia," said David Crunk, who received Pierce's heart 2 days after he died. Crunk had been waiting on a list for a year and a half.
"It brought tears to my eyes because I knew that I was going to still be here," said Crunk.
Crunk needed the transplant because of the damage experimental treatments caused when he was a boy.
"I wish he didn't do it," said Crunk. "I wish none of this happened to me or him." Crunk said he now considers the Gilbert's as family, often visiting them. They even gave him Pierce's Ford Mustang.

'Oh after everything you've done, I can thank you for how strong I have become.
Cause you brought the flames and you put me through hell,
I had to learn how to fight for myself. And we both know all the truth I could tell,
I'll just say this, is I wish you farewell. I hope you're somewhere praying.'
'Praying' - ⊠eshia

"He loved cars, like I love cars," said Crunk.

"Meeting the recipients was the light, the joy of this. They've all taken on aspects of Pierce," said Gilbert.

Gilbert has tattoos of the recipient's initials and the day Pierce passed in Roman numerals, handwriting from his suicide note and an EKG of Pierce's heartbeat after Crunk received his heart. Gilbert said her hope for writing the book is to end this epidemic and to bring the issue to light instead of sweeping it under the rug. "If I can prevent one suicide or convince one person to be an organ donor, then that's my legacy," said Gilbert. "Pierce's legacy was saving five lives."

So far, Gilbert said her book has received a great response and she's sold around 300 copies.

Several post from the end of the month:

Oddly ironic....a friend asked if I was aware that my book launched during suicide prevention month?

Ummm... nope. That'd be P's hand in all of this!

It really did not occur to me that my book came out during Suicide Prevention month, but I'm thrilled it did; since that is my purpose with the book, to help bring awareness to this epidemic!

Here's Mama Leslie with her stang back in the day.

This is for you P-diddy!

Elena, the reporter who interviewed me, texted to inform me that the producer of the morning show is going to contact me in regards to coming on the show to discuss my book! Luv, luv, luv KXII Channel 12 out of Sherman, Tx.

McKinney Bubble Life News story about my book:
A local mom from Whitewright penned a book about surviving her son's suicide in April of 2015.
The title, "Our Year of First Without You: A journey through suicide and organ donation," was written in hopes of promoting organ donation and shedding light on a dark, often unspoken subject — suicide.
We chose not to sweep the nature of our son's death under the rug, for what good would that do? For us, dying from suicide is no different than dying from any other disease. If no one speaks of it, then this epidemic will never end.
Our hope and prayer is to convince just one person from making this choice or to persuade just one to sign up to become an organ donor; thus, saving a life. If it can do that, then I will consider it successful and my legacy. Pierce's legacy was saving five lives with seven life-saving organs. The most one can donate is eight, so he was a near record breaker.
The book is a combination of stories about Pierce, our life, meeting the recipients, and surviving his decision of that night. It is rich with characters and is very raw — just a mom spewing out my thoughts. I am thankful for his buddies helping me fill some aspects I was unaware of at the time. I'm glad I posted monthly on Face Book to be able to recall that first year. I'm not the only contributing author, as there are postings from his first love in 8th grade, a note found at his grave from a former classmate, an English paper his best friend wrote as an assignment, and one his sister wrote as well.
The story is based on a toxic relationship that drove my son to make this choice. It discusses mental health, pressures facing our kids today and stats on organ donation and suicide.

Over Thanksgiving break, Morgan went to New Orleans with her cousin Emily. They had a great girls weekend and she loved seeing Jackson Square decked out for the holidays.

I found out Josh turned down a job offer in DC because he's holding out for one in DFW area. OH GEEZZZZ!!!!!! He said I better be worth it! No pressure there! Come on rich people, hire him as your personal chef!!!!!

Feeling blown away by this blessing! In the fall, we went to Love and War in Texas to see Two Tons of Steel and Justin Pecina. Justin dedicated P's favorite song, at the time of his passing, "She's The Cheating Kind" to him. After the show, Judy (David Ray's Mom) and I met Kevin Geil, lead singer for Two Tons of Steel. He asked if Judy was my mom; so, we explained how we knew each other. He was SHOCKED!! We had our picture taken with him and it's in the (first) book.

So, I e-mailed him requesting his address to send him a copy of the book since he's in it. He graciously gave me his address. Then, he sent me a download (via e-mail) of the yet to be released song - which is also the title of their new album, 'Gone.' WOW!!!!!
I think it needs to be retitled 'Gone (Pierce's song)'. He requested I not share it with many since it hasn't been released yet. The only people I shared it with was Tim, William, and Judy.

I hired a friend to create my website for my book it dawned on me, I really wanted 'Gone' on it. So, I e-mailed Kevin, asking when was the release date. He said mid to late February, due to it taking a while for a new album to launch. So, I told him I'd add it to the site once released. He said, no, go ahead and add it now! WOW!!!! How incredibly nice! I told him 'you are now officially my new favorite Texas music artist!!!!! Call up Wade Bowen and tell him to 'drink that Vodka' cuz he's now been replaced as my favorite Texas Country Music artist. He now holds the #2 spot!" #GodIsGreatAllTheTime

My post:

Celebrating my 2nd interview w/ KXII Ch. 12 in Sherman. Will air Sunday morning @ 6. Will also be on their site after it airs!! #TeamPierce #letsgoviralbaby #holdingittogetherwithducttapetissuesandyourprayers

While at a restaurant after my interview, I gave my card to a table of guys, who you could tell were co-workers and great friends. One of them said, 'Yeah, I thought I recognized you from TV and Facebook when you walked in.' Welp, now I guess I'm famous in Texoma! Look out Kathy Lee Gifford! I'm gunning for ya!

I spoke, for the 1st time, to my newly discovered 10 yr. old nephew and having him say, "Hi Aunt Bobbi' at the beginning of the conversation brought a HUGE smile to my face. Before getting off the phone with me, he asked if he can Skype with me this weekend because he wants to see me, Morgan and Uncle Tim while talking with us. I explained sure, for me and Morgan, because we'd be here decorating and watching college football on TV; but Uncle Timbo, goes hunting. He said he and his dad went once; but it didn't go so well, since they didn't see any animals. I told him not to worry, Timbo needs a new little boy to take hunting and he'd be sure he saw lots of animals! At the end, he said, 'Ok, I'll let you talk to my dad again.' I love you Aunt Bobbi.' Bio-half baby bro....bring him here and you're NEVER taking him back - just saying'!!! (Oh & sooooo polite too...it's obvious it's his mom's influence...not yours Josh!"

For each new morning with its light;
For rest and shelter of the night;
For health and food,
For love and friends;
For everything Thy goodness sends.⬚ - Ralph Waldo Emerson.
Happy Thanksgiving Yall⬚

December 2016:

Can't stop watching the last episode of 'This Is Us'. My heart continually breaks to pieces realizing that my half biological brother was raised under a lie that he was an only child.
I was blessed...Mommie Dearest gave me up to a great family; thus sparing me her wrath!! I just wish bio-bro bratty rat could have had escaped her wrath.
It's SOOOOOO weird to know, for once, I'm the oldest child!!!!
I've always been the youngest!! It's bizarre that I've met someone who has the EXACT same whacked out sense of humor as me...someone who always wants to be in touch. It's truly heartbreaking what Mommie-Monster Dearest did to him!!!

On the 2nd, my dear friends, Lisa H. and Robbin W. held a book-signing party for me in Lucas. I am so thankful for good friends have stuck with us, not run from us. We had a good turn out and it was nice seeing old neighbors.
My only regret of the holiday season being upon us is his

memories flooding back....yet, my motto: 1 step forward, 2 steps back! It's almost as if this 2nd Christmas seems harder than the first. I shared that on FB and a lady from California, who has mentored me through this since her son committed suicide four years prior to Pierce, said the same thing held true for them through their 2nd year of holidays.

Bullying leads Texas City senior to suicide
By Jake Reiner - Reporter
Posted: 6:53 PM, November 30, 2016
Updated: 4:21 PM, December 01, 2016
HOUSTON - Texas City High School senior Brandy Vela took her own life Tuesday afternoon.
Her family says despite being well-loved and having a lot of friends, none of it helped when it came to what they call the
"relentless bullying" that led to her eventual death.
Brandy Vela's final text to her family was: "I love you so much just remember that please and I'm so sorry for everything."
'David's Law' targets cyber-bullying
High school senior accused of bullying classmate into giving him over $6,000
Child cancer survivor kills herself over bullying EXCLUSIVE: Lauren Jauregui Taking a Break From Twitter, Opens Up About...
"I was the first one here," said Jacqueline Vela, Brandy's older sister, describing the last moments she had with her.
Jacqueline, 22, said she tried everything she could to save her 18-year-old sister Tuesday.
"I heard someone crying so I ran upstairs and I looked in her room and she's against the wall and she has a gun pointed at her chest and she's just crying and crying and I'm like, 'Brandy please don't, Brandy no,'" Jacqueline said.
Brandy's entire family tried to find the right words, but their troubled teen had already made up her mind.
"I was in my parents' room and I just heard the shot and my dad just yelled, 'Help me, help me, help me,'" Jacqueline recalled. Brandy shot herself in front of her parents and grandparents. Police said, she died at the hospital.
"I'm glad you got what you wanted. I hope this makes you happy," Victor Vela, 19, said, talking directly to the bullies he said targeted his younger sister.

'What if one of my organs
saves the life of someone who
finds the cure to cancer, or
something eⓍually profoundⓍ
-Author Unknown

Tim made the following post, along with these photos, which really meant a lot to me since he rarely, if ever, uses social media:

After what we've been through the past year and a half with the loss of our son, I am so incredibly proud of my wife for champion this cause, to save lives. She poured her heart and soul into writing, "Our Year of First Without You" A journey through suicide and organ donation. She feels if she can save just one life, either by preventing suicide or by getting someone to sign up to be an organ donor, then it will be successful. She hopes the book will answer the questions as to what led our son to make this choice. Her goal is to use part of the proceeds to accomplish her mission, to donate a book to every high school in Collin & Grayson Counties. And God willing, to all high schools in N. Texas or possibly even all of Texas. Ultimately, the entire US. You can purchase her book at her shopify account: MorganK-Publishing@myshopify.com

Please help us make this go viral!

Share this post on your wall.

Blessings,

Tim

A friend of mine, who is an attorney, posted this, along with a picture of my book: Sad to hear of the passing of Brian Loncar, a rather well known personal injury attorney in Dallas due to his "strong arm" ads for so many years. I'm wondering if he took his own life since it was about 1 week after his 16-year old daughter committed suicide. It's so vitally important to get the message out there that depression is an illness, not a weakness. I tip my hat to Bobbi Danice Morgan Gilbert for raising awareness about this issue, as well as organ donation, with her new book, now available on Amazon, "Our Year of First Without You".

P knew what he was doing picking your painting Brice McCasland,
for this message for us!!! ⊠BlessedBeyondMeasure

A Fallen Limb
A limb has fallen from the family tree
I keep hearing a voice that says 'Grieve not for me'
Remember the best times, the laughter, the song
The good life I lived, while I was strong.
Continue my heritage, I'm counting on you
⊠eep smiling and surely, the sun will shine through.
My mind is at ease, my soul is at rest.
Remembering all, now truly I was blessed.
Continue traditions, no matter how small.
Go on with your life, don't worry about falls.
I miss you all dearly, so keep up your chin.
Until the day comes were together again.
-Author Unknown

Terrific story⊠

Loving My Son, After His Death Ties
By NORA WONG DEC. 2, 2016

I can feel their unasked questions. People wonder how I can still stand, still walk, still laugh. But they don't ask. You can't ask that of a mother who has lost her child. My son, Daniel, died three years ago at the age of 22. When people ask me, "How… are you?," that pause, that inflection, tells me that's really what they want to know.

Broken Chain

We little knew that morning that
God was going to call your name.
In life we loved you dearly,
in death we do the same.

It broke our hearts to lose you,
you did not go alone;
for part of us went with you
the day God called you Home.

You left us peaceful memories,
your love is still our guide;
and though we cannot see you,
you are always at our side.

Our family chain is broken,
and nothing seems the same;
but as God calls us one by one,
the chain will link again.

Ron Tranmer

I am tempted to tell them that it is I who am lost, not he. I am lost in my search for him, knowing he is nowhere on this earth. And still, it would not surprise me if he were to appear by my side wearing only his jersey boxers eating a snack at the kitchen counter. At times I can almost smell his warm cheesy breath and his still-boyish sweat. But when I look over my shoulder, he is not there.

My mind invents stories. Daniel is not dead, he is lamenting the performance of his fantasy football team with high school buddies while they wait on line for ice cream at Magic-Mountain. HHe is in his dorm room at Stanford, talking deep into the night with his friends.

Daniel is lingering with new friends on the rooftop of his investment firm in Boston where he just started working.

"Where are you, Daniel?" I shout the question to the sky when I am strong enough to bear the silence that follows. "Why did you die?" Even that has no real answer. His doctors think Daniel died of new onset refractory status epilepticus, or Norse, a rare seizure disorder in which healthy people with no history of epilepsy suddenly begin to seize uncontrollably. The majority of patients die or survive with significant brain damage. There is no identified cause or established treatment for Norse. This cloud of uncertainty does not obscure what I know: My child is dead.

Your boy came to you with a heart full of love. He is with you still, and always. Thank you for reminding me of this truth.

The instinct to protect one's offspring runs through mothers of virtually all species. I violated the basic canon of motherhood. I failed to protect my child. That my child is dead while I still live defies the natural order.

I love my husband and our two surviving children, but I couldn't simply transfer my love for Daniel to them. It was for him alone. And so, for the longest time after his death, my love for Daniel bruised me.

So unbearable was my occluded heart that I called out to him in desperation one day: "What will I do with my love for you, Daniel?"

My eyes were closed in grief when suddenly I seemed to see him before me, his arms bent and lifted upward in supplication. In my mind's eye, his face was suffused with love and tinged with exasperation, a common look for Daniel.

Just love me, Mom, he says.

But where are you? I ask.

I'm here he answers with frustration. And then he is gone.

I had not heard his voice since the day before he suddenly fell ill. I spoke to him while he lay unseeing and unmoving in the hospital bed. I told him I loved him. I begged him to speak to me. I begged him to come back to me. He never answered or moved to squeeze my hand. The only flicker from him over his 79 days of hospitalization was a single tear. One day a tear slid from his left eye down his cheek and disappeared beneath his chin. And now, months after he had died, I felt him before me.

⊠ust love me, Mom. I'm here⊠

His words unleashed a torrent. I fell forward, my tears streaming. I felt breathless with release. I could continue to love him. I would love him in a new way. It was harder to do than I expected. I would see him everywhere, in every full moon, in each brilliant day. My spirits would soar. But there were days when a weight in my heart made each breath shallow and every step an effort. On the worst days I sit before my laptop and pour out my feelings to the only person who can take in my sorrow and remain unbowed. The keyboard is damp when the final refrain leaves my fingertips: I love you, Daniel, I love you. I miss you. I miss you. And then I press "send."

Daniel's friends continue to visit us. It is a pilgrimage of sorts. My heart tightens when I see them. Their presence illuminates our immeasurable loss. His friends reveal to me how much Daniel meant to them. Now there will be a missing groomsman at the wedding and empty air in the place of a steadfast friend. At the end of one visit, a young man asks, "Recognize this sweater?" I don't. "It's Daniel's," he explains. I suddenly recognize Daniel's old cotton sweater stretched to fit his friend. The young man folds forward to touch the sleeves of the sweater, hugging himself. He is tall and blond and athletic. He and Daniel were opposites in looks and temperament, best friends since nursery school. He had just returned from Moscow where he was working. "I wear this when I travel," he says, touching the arm of the sweater again. "It's so soft." I encourage Daniel's friends to tell me about their work and their plans for the future. At first they are self-conscious, and their voices are tender. They don't want to hurt me with their future plans when there is no future for Daniel. But as they speak of the things they will do and the places they will go, their excitement breaks free. I smile into the glow of their unlined, earnest faces and I feel my son. I think they feel him too. For a moment we are all reunited.

I will carry this child for the rest of my life. ***He lives within me, forever a young man of*** ⬚⬚. Others will carry him as they move forward in their lives. He will be with them when they look out to the world with compassion, when they act with determination and kindness, when they are brave enough to contemplate all the things in life that remain unknown.

I still search for him, but without desperation. I look for him in others. My search is lifted by his words: ⬚***ust love me. I'm here.***⬚

My post the following day:
I was so touched & honored to have received this from my dear friend's mom in Louisiana. We're truly blessed to have so many great, supportive friends in our life!

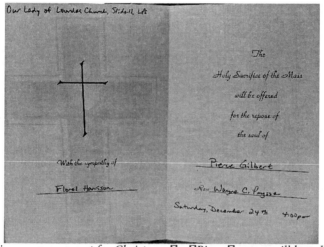

service announcement for Christmas ⬚*ve* ⬚*Pierce*⬚ *name will be called*

I sent my new nephews in Chicago their Christmas presents early since they won't be able to come visit us after Christmas. Luke lived in his sweat shirt for over a month! Luke is the oldest, followed by Conner, the red-head, like me, and Zach is the toddler.

> *'Saw ya standing there in the middle of thunder and lightening,*
> *I know you feel like you just can't win, but you're trying.*
> *It's hard to keep on, keeping on, when you're being pushed around,*
> *you don't even know which way is up, you just keep spinning down, round, down.*
> *Every storm runs, runs out of rain; just like every dark night turns into day.*
> *Every heartache will fade away, just like every storm runs, runs out of rain.'*
> *'Every Storm' - Gary Allan*

WOO-HOO!!!!!!! MY WEBSITE IS NOW LIVE!!!!! Special thanks to Kevin Gill from Two Tons of Steel for letting me use their new title song for their new album, that has yet to be released, Gone, for the back ground music! #blessedbeyondmeasure #TeamPierce #HeldTogetherWithDuctTapeTissuesAndPrayers

Finally having my website up and going was a huge relief! Once Lee launched it, he posted it on his Linkin account and within an hour, he had over 150 post-clicks on it. He said, "I really think this could turn out to be a huge thing Bobbi!"

> Even the strongest of us
> have moments
> when the burdens of life
> seem too great.
> It's then that the Lord
> whispers to our hearts...
> *Come to Me,*
> all you who are weary
> and burdened.
> and i will give you rest.
> MATTHEW 11:28 NIV

This was sent to me from Barry's son and it tells how badly things have gone wrong with some of the girls in our society today:

I have been reading your book the past couple of days, and I got to say it is very good. I had my own challenges with a girlfriend a year ago this month, and I had my run in with depression from it because like Pierce and Sarah were off and on, me and my ex-girlfriend were off and on, and if it wasn't for my dad, I probably wouldn't be sending this text message right now because I called him one night because she had broken-up with me and told me "I should just kill my-self" and I believed her because she had stressed me out and made me feel so bad about myself I actually believed her. So I called my dad in a last attempt effort to talk to someone, but I didn't tell him what was going on, but he could tell. So I can relate to Pierce and how he was feeling, this book has actually helped me with some of my issues I had about myself, so I just want to say thank you to you and Tim for sharing it with me, and I can tell Pierce was an awesome dude and I only wish I could have gotten to know him.

How could anyone say this to someone? I just cannot conceive the level of hatred in someone's heart to say this to another person. What has gone on in our society to lead our youth to ever utter these words, 'you should just kill yourself' to someone else?

On the 18th, we met the Karlin's for dinner in Plano. Race, who was Pierce's best friend from Princeton, was home from college for Christmas break, so he came along. It was so great seeing them again and catching up! Biggest surprise of the night was Race wearing boots! Pierce ALWAYS tried to talk him into buying some and he never did, but now he wears them proudly!

On the 19th, we held our annual ugly Christmas sweater party. David Ray – P's heart recipient was the judge.

The winners of the contest were Mayor Jim Olk of Lucas and his lovely wife Joy!

LaDeaux is demanding a recount on tonight's vote!

My cousin messaged me saying she ordered a copy of the book for her friend. Her son drove to his girl friends house last night & shot himself in her driveway. PEOPLE!! WE HAVE TO FIND A WAY TO END THIS EPIDEMIC!!!!! Make a pledge with me now that in 2017, we will ban together, demand change in our schools and in the form of legislation, to protect our kids!!!!

In mid-December, I went to get my angel's wing tattoo. Not sure what I was thinking getting them on the side of my hip – it hurt so bad I thought I was going to pass out! Towards the end, one of the guys at the shop walked in and asked if Rano was killing me and I said "Yes, I think I'm going to pass out!" Rano's reply was 'well, pass out in your car because I'm done!'

We held our annual company Christmas party at a restaurant in Allen. We invited all our employees and subs. We had a great turnout and are blessed to have them as a part of our team!

our annual Christmas card

Hey, I hope it's sunny where ever you are,
but that's sure not the picture tonight in my car,
and it sure ain't easing my pain, all the songs like,
'Rainy ⬚ ight in Georgia', ⬚entucky Rain', 'Here Comes That Rainy Day
Feeling Again', 'Blues Eyes Crying In The Early Morning Rain';
they go on an on, and there's no two the same.
Oh it would be easy to blame all theses songs about rain⬚
Well, I thought I was over you, but I guess maybe I'm not⬚
'Songs About Rain' - Gary Allan

We went to the Stockyards in Ft. Worth to see Kasey Musgrave's Christmas special at Billy Bob's. We were upgraded to the celebrity suite when she decided not to stay the night, but to head home instead. Of course, at mid-night, it was the 22nd; and thus, in typical fashion, I couldn't sleep. So, I went into the living room area and watched TV.

At 3:15 (of course, P's perfect timing) while praying, that's when it finally happened. I was finally able to forgive Sarah (not that she'll ever know). I finally realized, while yes, she played a HUGE role in Pierce's decision to take his own life, I do not believe, in her heart, that was her intent. It felt good to reach this point and it was helpful in my healing process to achieve this moment.

I made the decision after that, to contact the detective who worked Pierce's case. I wanted/needed to see his letter he left for her. I have always been a 'needle in the haystack' type of person, who cannot leave a stone unturned. So the next morning, I contacted him, requesting to see it. He questioned 'why now? Did I have a therapist? What did my therapist think of me seeing it?' I explained that I had reached the point of finally being able to forgive her and that for my healing process, I needed to see it. I said yes, I have a therapist; but no, I have not asked her opinion on this matter.

He agreed to meet with me the next afternoon if he didn't get called out on a case. I meet my friend Lisa for lunch before-hand. She said she would go with me if I needed her. I told her I thought I could handle going alone. She expressed, after I told her I finally forgave Sarah, that I need to write another book since so much continues to happen in regards to Pierce and our life after Pierce.

I met with the detective around 3:30 that afternoon. I took him 5 copies of my book, one for him personally, and the other copies for him to give to families he works with who experience suicide.

We visited for a while and he expressed that he was happy I came in since; they only ever see the events of that moment – not the after effects, of years later. He inquired how Morgan was doing, recalling how hurt and angry she was after losing her brother. That really touched me – him recalling that and expressing that he cared about our daughter.

He shared after my call, he went back and pulled Pierce's file to review the letter since it had been over a year; he had forgotten, what was in it. He said, "all in all, considering, it's not a bad letter." He asked if I wanted to be alone when I viewed it. I told him no, it was okay for him to stay with me. When he handed me the envelope, he apologized that the paper it was written on was dirty due to them having to dust it for finger prints. I pulled the folded 8 ☒ x 11 paper out of the envelop, unfolded it and was surprised by what I read and re-read, several times.

I asked the detective if I could have a copy of it. He sat silent for a few minutes and said, "No ma'am, I'm sorry. I gave my word that I would never release it. I know that may anger you, seeing that I told her and her mom that, but I have to respectfully ask that you let me honor my word. I told him it's okay and I respect him for honoring his word.

In reality, I don't need a copy of it because I have it burned into my brain. At first, I was going to keep what it said private, just for Tim, Morgan and myself; but, I have decided to share it because I'm very proud of the boy I raised and it helps to complete his story. It was written on an 8 /12 x 11 copier paper. The first 3/4 was in black sharpie, then he drew a line across the page, drew an outline of a black heart in the bottom left corner, and the bottom 1/4 was written in ink. I'm guessing he wrote the top part here and the last part on the way there.

On the top in sharpie:
I hope your happy with your new boyfriend in Melissa, Tx.
My blood is on your hands now.

On the bottom in ink:
All I ever did was love you. Nothing I ever did
was good enough for you. I hope your happy now.
It's okay, I'm looking forward to seeing Paul.

WOW! Just WOW!!! It shows he was just DONE!!!!! There was not the anger or the hate filled harsh words I expected. If it were me, I would have called her EVERY name in the book; but, he didn't. While heartbreaking, I couldn't be more proud of him. He was sick and tired of getting his heart broke continually. Done being jerked around!

This year, we decided to start a new tradition of staying home on Christmas Eve, instead of driving to see family. Morgan came home for break and announced that 'she would be staying with Jenn & Britt since they have young kids, it seems more like Christmas than our empty house.' Sigh....once again, she's not calling a spade a spade! So, they came over Christmas Eve and we had our traditional Mexican food for dinner. We had a great time; it was, for me, surprisingly enjoyable. I love our family and tradition; but with all the kids growing up, having families of their own, things have not been the same for several years, even prior to Pierce's passing.

SATURDAY, DECEMBER 24 CHRISTMAS EVE

4:00 pm

Dottie Lyons, Robert Calogero Sr.,
Johnny Gordon, Louis Collignon,
Larry Chabert, Thomas Chabert,
Aurelia Chabert, Gertrude Chabert,
Lena Sandrock, Harry Sandrock,
Stephanie Sandrock, Henry Sandrock,
Margaret Catton, Grace Segretto,
Elizabeth Mangiaracina, Mary Russo,
Joseph Cervini, Josephine Cervini,
Chet Ballex, Otis Favre Sr., Suzi Hebert,
The Faciane & Hebert Families,
Solomon Harrison, Danny Faciane,
Patricia Williams-Graves, Don Offner,
Adam & Lena Faciane, Ubert Labat,
Pierce Gilbert, Jerry Breland,
Bryan Appe, Dudley Vandenborre,
Verna Englert, Rose Cimino,
Bertha Firmin, James Firmin Sr.,
Thomas Firmin, Joseph Nelson,
Thelma Godwin, Catherine Godwin,
Frost Godwin Jr., Int. of Patrick Smith

6:30 pm

Kevin Brewer, Fr. Hotard, Fr. Hall,

Midnight

Fr. Grenham, Fr. Frank, Bob Hansen
OLL Parishioners

Copy of service program

My friend Lisa sent this to me. It's from Pierce's mass in Slidell, Louisiana. The Christmas Eve Mass calls out all lost souls from that year. Her Mom requested Pierce's name b added to the list. I had originally planned on attending, but after decorating for the holidays, my back has been bothering me and getting worse; so, a long car ride would not be good for me. It is such a HUGE blessing to us that we have friends, who count us as family, that would do this for us!

'It's bittersweet to look back now
at memories withered on the vine,
but just to hold you close to me, for a moment in time.
I would have loved you anyway
I'd do it all the same;
Not a second I would change,
Not a touch I would trade,
Had I known how my heart would break,
I'd've loved you anyway'
'I Would Have Loved You Anyway' - Trisha Yearwood

As I look back at this pic taken Christmas Eve, I admire it. The other night, Tim looked back on a photo I posted of Morgan with Tux (her horse), taken shortly after we bought him, said, 'God must surely have a plan for us; but, it's really been hard on us' - meaning how severely it has changed/aged us in the process. And, yes, he is SO correct in this evaluation.

But, there's the flip side of this, we're still standing! We are still able to find happiness. We are still able to put one foot in front of the other. We are still able to make new memories, while cherishing the past. We are still hopeful for the future.
GOD IS GREAT, ALL THE TIME!
#HeldTogetherWithDuctTapeTissuesAndPrayers#TeamPierce

When I was decorating for Christmas, I decided to get all new decorations so I could be excited again for Christmas. The only three things I kept are: our stockings my mom made for us, my nativity, and our quilted advent calendar mama made. I had to make a decision – do I put out Pierce's stocking or not. I decided to and ended up putting LaDeaux's toys in it (sorry about ya P, but the Deaux needs a stocking!).

My nephew in Chicago opened his last gift from me. It's Pierce's first lacrosse jersey when he played for Allen in 5th grade. It still shocks me how much he looks like Pierce!

This pic popped up in my memories from 7 years ago. I love this because it shows the love and friendship they had for one another!

*'It's hard describing a heartache, aww, cuz it's a one of a kind of a thing,
serious injury and a whole lot of pain, if it were a storm,
I'd compare it to a hurricane, oh its even got a name. If it were a drink,
it'd be a strong one; if were a sad song, it would be a long one.
If it was a color, it'd be deep, deep, blue; but, if we're talking about a
heartache, it would be you.'
'It Would Be You' - Gary Allan*

Josh, Michelle, Cierra, and Zach arrived on the 26th. The two middle boys stayed with their grandmother. While I would have loved to of had them here; there were some adult things we needed to discuss, being that this was our first time together. They flew into Love Field. I greeted them with a sign that said 'Bratty Rat Bio-Bro' and I was dressed as cousin Eddy from the movie 'National Lampoon's Christmas Vacation'. I took them to eat at Mother & Daughter's in Dallas. I brought with me their Christmas gifts, so they opened them while we were there.

One of Josh's gifts was a duplicate of Pierce's cross necklace. After they were done, I took out of my purse a pamphlet and handed it to Josh, saying, "Oh yeah, I forgot one more thing." He looked at it and it didn't register to him what it was. I said, "After your interview today in Ft. Worth, Tim will be picking you up and you'll be going to the lease with him to go hunting. He was so happy he teared up!

Really??? Brat tears up over going hunting, but not the cross necklace! His wife and I coordinated it, with her sneaking in the items he need to bring with him in his luggage, to go hunting! She also provided me all his info so I would be able to buy him his out-of-state hunting license.

While they were gone to the lease, we had some great girl time together. I showed them around Ft. Worth the first day. The second day, I took them to old downtown McKinney for lunch and shopping.

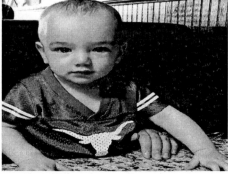

my cute lunch date

We hung out at the house the third day and Tim and Josh returned that evening. Josh sat in the first blind Pierce ever sat in the first time he got a buck. He used Pierce's deer rifle and he got his first buck! Josh had been hunting several years ago, but only shot two doe. He was so happy and Tim said he didn't want to come back.

The next day was New Year's Eve. We drove to the cemetery to see Pierce's headstone. I could tell it was starting to bother Josh, so I said, "Okay, everybody load-back up! Time for lunch!" We took them to eat chicken fried steak @ Cattleman's in Blue Ridge. Being from Chicago, Michelle and Cierra had never heard of it; much less, eaten it. I had to explain to them what it was on the way to the restaurant. They both liked it (of course)!

At one point, Josh went back into the house. I assumed he was just getting something to drink. When I came in a few minutes later to get more wine, he handed me his phone, saying, "Here, look at what I just sent your mom."
I said, "you didn't send my mom anything because you don't know her number! You may have sent YOUR MOM something , but not mine!"
He said, 'just read it!"
"I can't because I don't have my glasses on. Just read it to me."
He cleared his throat and read, "I'm in Texas at my sister's house. We just returned from your dead grandson's grave. How you cannot want to have anything to do with her or her beautiful family is beyond me! You are pure evil! Never speak to me again!"
Then he just started sobbing. I gave him a hug and said, "It's okay, we don't need her. Well, you might, she is your mom; but, she's not mine. Eventually, as a Christian, you are going to have to decide if you can forgive her or not; but, that decision doesn't have to be made right now."

Tim teaching Cierra how to shoot the 22 rifle. She was a good shot!

That evening, friends of ours came to dinner and we shot off fireworks. It was a great way to ring in the New Year!

Zack looks like he could be Tim's son!

The secret of life isn't knowing what to do or say,
it's simply showing up and being there.
-Author Unknown

January 2017

They were originally scheduled to fly out the following day, but their flight was canceled. The next available flight was in three days. The next day, I took them to Ft. Worth to eat at Joe T Garcia's. Mama and my friend Shani met us for lunch. After, we took them to the Stockyards, to the White Elephant Saloon, the Stockyards Hotel, and Billy Bob's. I told him it was rude of him to have his butt mounted without any pants on! So of course, he had to pose for a picture!

Brat at the Stockyards Hotel

'Life ain't always beautiful, sometimes it can break your heart.
Life ain't always beautiful, you think you're on your way,
and it's just a dead end road, at the end of the day.

But the struggles make you stronger, and the changes make you wiser.
And happiness has it's own way, of taking it's sweet time.

So life ain't always beautiful, tears will fall sometimes.
So life ain't always beautiful, but it's a beautiful ride.'
'Life Ain't Always Beautiful' - Gary Allan

The next day, I dropped them off at the airport. As I was hugging Zach good-bye, Michelle snapped this picture.

A few post from January:

So, January never lets me down.
In typical fashion, it has delivered.
The let-down.
You get through the holidays (this year they were a mixed bag of great new traditions and somehow, harder than the first without P).
Then you pack up the decorations and settle back into reality....
REALITY....hit today....
He's not here.
He's not coming back.
The saddness.
The heartache
The what-ifs.
The what will never be.
The missed opportunity.
The missed traditions.
The hopes.
The plans.

One step forward and two steps back.
#HeldTogetherWithDuctTapeTissuesAndPrayers

On the 13th, Morgan and I went into town to run errands and have lunch before she returned to college for her spring semester. We had a great few weeks together and we're going to miss her!

Josh received a text message from Jody, Mommie Dearest's husband, asking what was going on? Why had they not heard from him or the kids during the holidays and why had Jan not yet mailed their gifts? Josh replied that he spent the holiday's at his big sister's house in Texas. The big sister she gave up 48 years ago – two years prior to his birth. He then said, "Yeah, ask your wife about that and see what she says!" Jody replied that he was in shock! They were on vacation visiting friends, but would ask her about it on the drive home.

'Farewell fine people, we'll meet again,
in a better time and place. Look towards the Heavan,
when I cross your mind, and you just might see my face.
On a cloud, on a cloud,
on a cloud, lookin' down.'
'On A Cloud' – Cross Canadian Ragweed

My post:
Anyone with siblings - make this your status and answer honestly!

1) The smartest? Me cuz if it's Brat, Lord help us!
2) Better lookin'? Duh! Me cuz have you actually seen Josh!!??
3. Most sensitive? josh cuz he hasn't come out of the closet yet according to Morgan
4. Best driver? Me cuz I make Michele sick!!!!!
5. More social? Me cuz josh hasn't come out of the closet y
6. Most stubborn? Me cuz I ALWAYS get my way!!!!!!
7. Who's dad's favorite? Don't know cuz Jan can't seem to remember who our dads are!!!!!!!!!
8. Who's liable to fight anyone? Little Z cuz I'm raisin' him right!!!!
9. Who's a better singer? Brat - just cuz he needs to be right f somethin'
10. Better cook? Me cuz josh is an imposter chef wanna be!!!!!!!
11. Clothes And shoe Hoarder? Me cuz josh is poor!!!!!!
12. Who wears the most Hats? Me cuz I ROCK at multi-tas
13. Who was the baddest kid? Josh cuz Jan raised
14. Who has the biggest home? Josh cuz he thinks life is a contest!!!!!!
15. Who was born 1st? Me (although josh just found out!SUX to josh - just sayin'!!!!!!!!!!!!!!!!!)
16. Who is better at sports? Me cuz I actually watch them vs. Josh's ass!!!!!!!!
17. Best hair? Josh cuz he uses Rogain!!!!!
18. Most kids? Josh cuz he's never heard of condums!!!!!!!
19. Coffee Drinker? Michele vs. Josh (the jury is still out!!!!!) But, Tim was concerned for his Kurge durin' yalls stay!!!!!!!
20. Most expensive taste? Josh cuz that happens to kids who grew poor with a mom who used all her money on plastic surgery, but hell, if I looked like her too, I would have too!!!!!!!!
21. Tallest? Josh, cuz he's the jolly green giant wanna be!!!!
22. Biggest Disney fanatic? C - cuz she lives in fantasy world!!!

Needless to say, I've never heard from her again and the only contact Josh has had with her is when she mailed Luke a birthday gift in May.

Received this message last night:
Mrs. Gilbert,
I saw posts on Face book about your book and decided to purchase it. I grew up in the Lovejoy district. I know of your daughter because I was really good friends with Robert B. and Kate in early high school. I transferred out of Lovejoy after my sophomore year because I was being bullied and became depressed. Thankfully I have amazing parents who refused to watch me suffer and decided to take action and help me overcome my issues. Your book and your words have inspired me to be more vocal and speak up about issues of depression and anxiety! I hope I can inspire people just as you have by writing this book!!!
I deeply admire what you are setting out to do by writing this book. I got it today and finished reading it today. I couldn't put it down. It was truly inspiring. I just wanted to reach out and thank you for speaking up and not pushing issues of depression under the rug like society likes to do. Just like you, I shared my story at my new high school my senior year in hopes that maybe someone listening and struggling would seek help because me, along with other students, spoke out about their experiences with bullying in relation to depression. I thought I'd share the video with you. Thanks again for speaking out and sharing your story! It has touched my heart!!

You can view Olivia's video on YouTube. The title is **MNHS PALS 'If you only knew me'** Campaign 2014. IT IS VERY POWERFUL and I wish all schools would show it every year, starting in sixth grade.

> *Farewell fine people, we'll meet again,*
> *in a better time and place.*
> *Look towards the Heaven, when I cross your mind,*
> *and you just might see my face.*
> *On a cloud, on a cloud,*
> *on a cloud, lookin' down.'*
> *'On A Cloud' – Cross Canadian Ragweed*

Her post from the 22nd:
I was touched after reading Mrs. Gilbert's book about her son's suicide. I reached out to her and she shared my story too! I'm so thankful for people like Bobbi Danice Morgan Gilbert who aren't afraid to speak up about things people don't typically want to talk about! If you haven't read the book, I highly recommend it. Thank you for touching my heart!!!

On the 31st, Mark Lackey, Pierce's best friend from MCA, came to visit us! It was so great seeing him and his parents again! It's funny to see him all grown up!

Depression isn't always suicide notes and pill bottles. Sometimes it's all smiles and fake laughter. Depression isn't always easy to notice. @In loving memory of Jason.S.Hearn

Great blog I read:

To the mom hiding in her bathroom, needing peace for just one minute, as the tears roll down her cheeks..

To the mom who is so tired she feel likes she can't function anymore and would do anything to lay down and get the rest she needs...

To the mom sitting in her car, alone, stuffing food in her face because she doesn't want anyone else to see or know she eats that stuff...

To the mom crying on the couch after she yelled at her kids for something little and is now feeling guilty and like she is unworthy... To the mom that is trying desperately to put those old jeans on because all she really wants is to look in the mirror and feel good about herself...

To the mom that doesn't want to leave the house because life is just too much to handle right now...

To the mom that is calling out for pizza again because dinner just didn't happen the way she wanted it to...

To the mom that feels alone, whether in a room by herself or standing in a crowd...

You are enough.

You are important.

You are worthy.

This is a phase of life for us. This is a really, really hard, challenging, crazy phase of life.

In the end, it will all be worth it. But for now it's hard. And it's hard for so many of us in many different ways. We don't always talk about it; but, it's hard and it's not just you.

You are enough.

You are doing your best.

Those little eyes that look up at you - they think you are perfect. They think you are more than enough.

Those little hands that reach out to hold you - they think you are the strongest.

They think you can conquer the world.

Those little mouths eating the food you gave them - they think that you are the best because their bellies are full.

Those little hearts that reach out to touch yours - they don't want anything more. They just want you. Because you are enough. You are more than enough, mama. You. Are. Amazing. -Bethany Jacobs

February 2017

A dear friend, who was one that ran to us, not from us, & has been a constant, shared this w/ me today. Luv it!

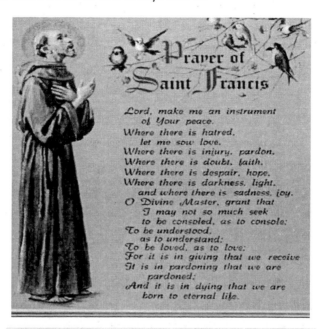

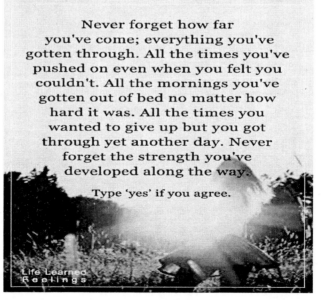

On the 3rd, we went with our friends, The Van Riper's, to see Eric Church at American Airlines Center in Dallas. It was an AMAZING concert! When he played 'Give Me Back My Hometown' I recorded it and posted it, saying P – this is for you from Eric!

My post from the 6th:
(accompanied by the video of him laughing 2 weeks prior to his death)
It's so uttterly surereal.....
that I can become transfixed by a snip-it of a video.....
that I desperately become transfixed on it....
that I don't want to stop watching it.....
that's the missing you...
that's the part that...
no matter what...
will never....
come hell or high water.....
will NEVER go away.
It's ok......
It's ok so long as you acknowledge this truth...
As long as YOU ARE WILLING to be okay with this...
If not, I'm sorry....but while I'm still healing, I can't be a part of trying to help you heal.

There are MANY professionals out there to help you.
PLEASE REACH OUT & SEEK HELP

God's Gift

We give our loved ones back to God.
And just as He first gave them to us,
and did not lose them in the giving.
So we have not lost them,in returning them to Him,
for life is eternal, love in immortal, death is only a horizon, and
a horizon is nothing, but the limit of our earthly sight.
- Author Unknown

Kyle O'Brien would often give the same answer to those who asked him how he was doing. "I can't complain. I'm still alive."

But Feb. 7, Kyle's brothers, friends, acquaintances, family and more gathered in front of the Delta Upsilon house to mourn his unexpected death Feb. 3 in Oklahoma City.

Kyle, who OU listed as a finance sophomore, visibly impacted the lives of the 20 or so men who memorialized him Tuesday night with tear-filled speeches and stories. He was described as a nice, goofy, happy and caring person — one speaker said he had "an aura that was inescapable and contagious."

"Each day that me, Mac and Justin would be getting ready to go work out at the (Sarkeys Fitness Center), we play some music pretty loud, and obviously he could hear it in his room," said Kody Fagin, one of Kyle's fraternity brothers who lived next to him.

"And for some reason in Kyle's room they had this huge hole in the wall," Fagin said. "And Kyle had this portable speaker and he would put it into the wall and blast the most random music to try and drown out our music." It became almost a daily habit. Another DU brother had been in talks with Kyle to study abroad with him and to start a company together. He recalled Kyle writing "You miss 100 percent of the shots you don't take" on the wall each time before he studied, except he'd attribute it not to Wayne Gretzky, but to Michael Scott from "The Office."

"(Kyle was) the best person I've ever known," he said. "We'll all live much better lives because of that man."

Many remembered Kyle's love for the New York Jets. If Kyle was guarding someone when he himself was playing football, he would tell his opponents they were on "O'Brien Island," a spin on the Darrelle Revis-trademarked saying.

He took pride that the team, which has had one winning season since 2011, would often have a higher draft pick than most other teams. Even more than the Jets, many others' memories of Kyle revolved around sports. One of Kyle's fraternity "littles" recalled a time when Kyle hit a drive on the golf course like Adam Sandler in "Happy Gilmore." Jack Slay, another of Kyle's brothers, said he and Kyle once ran a 5K without training for it. Another said Kyle often pestered him to get lacrosse sticks so they could play together — something he never did. "I sort of wish I could play lacrosse with him right now."

He danced to make people laugh. He was there for another brother after his grandmother died, even offering to drive him to Dallas to be with family. He was there for seemingly everyone.

Attendees, once everyone had shared their memories, lit candles in honor and in remembrance of Kyle. Then, slowly, after a period of deep thought and prayer, they disappeared.

At the vigil, Kyle's father, William, said his funeral will be at 11:30 Feb. 11 at the St. Francis of Assisi Catholic Church in Grapevine, Texas.

Much is still unknown about the manner of Kyle's death. Oklahoma City Police are investigating a suspicious death from Friday night in which the body of a man in his 20s was found at the base of a parking garage, but it is unconfirmed whether the two situations are linked.

 ---From the OU Daily

Suicide rates for college students, especially freshman, is at an epidemic level. Our universities need to do more to help protect our student's mental health.

On the 8th, Mark started to work for Pierce Remodeling Group. We know P is beyond thrilled & smiling down on all of us from Heaven above!!!!!

Tim and I went to lunch that day and when we returned back to the ranch, Tim said, "Wow! P's with us – big time! He's really happy about Mark working for us!" I sent a text to his mom that the next day and she said Mark could sense Pierce with him all that first day; and, he was so proud to be wearing the shirt with his name on it!

On the 8th, I found out my book, which I donated to several schools in our area in the fall, was not in the library. I was livid! So I penned a letter to the editor of several papers:

As a grieving mother, I penned a book "Our Year of First Without You" 'A journey through suicide and organ donation'; to bring suicide to the forefront, in hopes of spreading awareness and preventing someone else from making the same same choice my 17 yr. old son made 19 months ago.

'The art is not one of forgetting, but letting go.
And when everything else is gone, you can be rich in loss.'
-Rebecca Solnit

Part of the proceeds are to be applied to help me accomplish my mission, of donating a book to every high school in the N.Tx. area, and God willing, all of Texas, or even possibly the entire US.

I donated books to local schools first, before the holidays. Imagine my dismay when a family friend of ours; who works for Trenton HS, found out this week it was not in the library. When she questioned the asst. librarian about it, she said, 'Oh well, the counselor is reading it now, but it's been passed around most of the staff so far.' She then approached the head librarian who stated that she had 'scanned the book and found it inappropriate for children.'

WHAT??? It's not as if I'm trying to donate it to the elementary school library. So, it begs the question, just what are the high school students in Trenton allowed to read - Dr. Seuss?

Then, her daughter, who attends Whitewright HS came home saying it's not in their library either. A friend of my son's inquired about it in the office and the principal said, "I do not find it appropriate for kids; therefore, it will not be allowed in my school." Sir, last time I checked, the high school is not a business; therefore, it is not YOUR SCHOOL. Actually, it's the TAX PAYERS school. Along with your salary, and the superintendents, being footed by the TAX PAYERS!

So, let's examine this further….all I know of personally is that in the past nine years, Whitewright HS has had 8 deaths to suicide. But, you are choosing NOT to let in a book that can shed first-hand experience and light onto the subject because I'm assuming you think 'it will put ideas in the student's heads.'

So, rather than try to help the students; which last time I checked, that IS ACTUALLY YOUR JOB, you'd rather bury your head in the sand and pray it doesn't happen again. Yeah….that formula seems to be working out great so far; in a town of 1,604 you have 8 suicides in 9 years of teens, maybe it's time to try a new tactic.

Take for example, Chico ISD. Not only did they ALLOW the book into their high school library, but also their MIDDLE school library. Keep in mind, it's probably because they are actually EDUCATED on the facts that suicide is the FOURTH leading cause of death for ages 10 -14!!!!!!! And as, we all seem to know here - 2nd leading cause of death for 15 - 24 year olds.

Why is it public schools can teach LGBTQ courses....but not suicide.
Why is it public schools will let MADD stage HORRIFIC reenactments of an auto wreck due to drunk driving before prom, but - SHHHHH - NOT SUICIDE.
Oh I know, at the end of the year, y'all eventually get around to having a talk for 30 minutes or so about it.
Good for you, check off that box. Call me crazy, but shouldn't that 'talk' happen at the BEGINNING of the school year; possibly in September, which is suicide awareness month? Wouldn't that talk be MORE IMPACTFUL if survivors of an actual suicide shared their stories.
But, no, please keep doin' it the way we always have and just sit back, relax, and when the next
teen takes their life....call in the grief counselors, say a prayer and move on to next year.
- Bobbi Gilbert, Author/Guest Speaker/Advocate for ALL OUR CHILDREN
PROUD Mother of Bobby Pierce Forest Gilbert 2/24/98 - 4/20/15

In total contrast, a friend posted the following article to my wall the next day. BRAVO WYLIE ISD!!!!!!!
LOCAL HIGH SCHOOL TACKLES SENSATIVE ISSUES:
Students and teachers in the Wylie East High School theatre department decided to go ahead with two plays that cover the difficult subject of suicide even after a suicide attempt happened the week before on the Wylie East campus. They decided it was too important to ignore.
"And we should be doing this. And we should be talking to our kids about it," said Wylie East High School Theatre Director Andrea Farnham.
The performances took place in the school's small Black Box Theater last week. The first called "I Don't Want To Talk About It" presented a series of monologues and scenes confronting a variety of teen issues including rumors, bullying, and suicide. The second play called "What I Want to Say But Never Will" offers a glimpse into a teen's private thoughts.

> *'She's fine, most of the time, she takes her days with a smile.*
> *She moves like, dancing in the light,*
> *spinning around to the sound, sometimes she falls down.*
> *Breath, just breath, take the world off your shoulders, put it on me.*
> *Breath, just breath, let the life that you led, be all that you need. Let*
> *go of the fear, let go of the time,*
> *let go of the ones that try to put you down.*
> *You're gonna be fine, don't hold it inside,*
> *if you hurt right now, then let it all out.'*
> *-'Breath' Ryan Star*

January 26th a male student was found in a school bathroom during the lunch hour. Initial reports from the school said he "attempted to harm himself."

He was found by other students. Paramedics responded and rushed to the student to the hospital. He survived but is still recovering from his injuries.

The school plays had already been in the works for several weeks and Farnham says they immediately considered canceling them out of respect for the student and the sensitive nature of the subject.

But, instead, teachers, students, and school administrators decided they should continue.

"We didn't want to offend anybody. And we didn't want to make anybody uncomfortable," said Farnham. "We talked with administration and they said no, this is important. You should be doing this."

The students agreed. And last Thursday night went ahead with the two performances hoping they brought attention, to both students and their parents, to the variety of issues that today's teenagers face.

"Sometimes people just get wrapped up and things don't end well. Or people just get overwhelmed," said senior Savannah Aguilar.

"It's hard to go through things when you feel alone and feel like you can't talk to anybody," said junior Carissa Thatcher.

"And a lot of people think oh this could never happen to my child my brother or sister or best friend or anybody I know. But we don't know who it could be," added senior Gemma Warren.

"It gives a voice to everyone, to people who keep those dark emotions inside," said sophomore Andrew Barlow who plays the role of a bullied teen whose character opts to end his life. "You get a feeling how everyone is attacking and it does feel overwhelming at times," he said of the experience on stage. "And it is scary, and it's sad."

"You don't know if a kid is really struggling with something because they may not show that," added Carissa Thatcher.

"Talk about this sort of thing more often," Gemma Warren recommended. "because a lot of times parents and adults don't talk about this sort of thing until something drastic happens." "And that's the biggest thing is that we need to talk more. Because every kid feels this way. Every kid feels this way, some insecurity, something is bothering them," said Farnham.

"And if we notice a little bit of angst and anxiety in there we need to pry just a little bit, to make sure they really are OK." Because if all the world's a stage, the youngest players need the rest of us…to listen.   Copyright 2016 WFAA

I wish more schools would take this approach. I have often said; if we're not talking about it with our teens, removing the stigma attached to it, then how are they going to know to ask for help? How are they going to know how to describe how they are feeling? They often feel alone – like they are the only one dealing with these feelings/issues. We've de-stigmatized the word sex; by it being so continually in our faces, through media – rather TV, music videos, publications, or movies. I propose we do the same. Let's talk about it so much, it's not 'taboo' or 'off limits' or 'a secret!'

If you've ever attended a funeral and no one is discussing the cause of death, it's suicide. When you die from depression, it's suicide. As I tell student's in my speeches, SUICDE IS A PERMANENT SOLUTION TO A TEMPORARY PROBLEM!

I Did ⬚ot Die

Do not stand at my grave and weep;
I am not there, I do not sleep.
I am a thousand winds that blow.
I am the diamond glints on snow.
I am the sunlight on ripened grain.
I am the gentle autumn rain.
When you awaken in the morning's hush;
I am the swift uplifting rush
Of ⬚uiet birds in circled flight;
I am the soft stars that shine at night.
Do not stand at my grave and cry;
I am not there, I did not die.
-Anonymous

On the 9th, my interview with KTEN aired at 6 p.m.

"We've got to stop it," Mother writes book about her son's suicide Posted: Feb 09, 2017 5:19 PM CST

WHITEWRIGHT, TX- A Whitewright mother is sharing her struggle of going through life after her son committed suicide. The Gilbert family has been open about the struggles with depression their 17- year old son Pierce Gilbert had before taking his own life in 2015.

Now they're sharing their story with a book in hopes of saving another family from dealing with this tragedy.

Bobbi Gilbert still remembers the last hours she saw her son Pierce alive. "Me and him and Tim sat in the media room and watched the ACM Awards. We were all laughing and joking together," said his mother Bobbi Gilbert. During the early morning hours of April 20th 2015, Pierce snuck- out of the house and drove to an ex- girlfriend's home where he took his own life.

"He took off his cross necklace, his class ring and hung it on the back trailer hitch and stood in her yard and shot himself," said Gilbert. Forever brokenhearted, Gilbert says she didn't want her son's memory to fade.

She says too many people suffer from depression which can lead to suicide.

"For 15 to 24 year olds, it's the second leading cause of death. We've got to put a stop to it," said Gilbert.

In a book written by Gilbert she talks about her family's struggle with Pierce's death in hopes of keeping another family from feeling this type of pain.

"I want people to get that there is hope. That you can survive it. I want people to learn to be aware of the signs, realize they need to get help and that help is available; especially, for our teens, " said Gilbert. Along with teaching others about teen suicide Gilbert also talks about the importance organ donation. Pierce helped save five lives.

"I received the left kidney and a pancreas," said recipient Alicia Slimak. 'I know feel like the Gilbert's are my family. When I met Morgan, I told her ' I can not replace your brother, but now you have a sister.'

On a mission to change lives, Gilbert says though it's taken the life of her son, knowing her story can save one family helps heal the pain. Anyone interested in purchasing the book and learning more about the donor recipients, you can purchase the book on Amazon or at morgank-publishing.myshopify.com. The book is available for both Kindle and Nook.

On the 10th, someone following me on FB posted this to my wall (along with a picture of the book):

'I'm reading this book now and every page makes me cry. Just reading it is inspiring.'

Receiving positive feedback like this really encourages me to keep forging ahead; especially after set-backs, (like finding out some of the schools didn't put the book in their libraries because Cindy, Sarah's mom, called all the local schools, saying she has a law suit against me, it's all lies and she'll sue them if they put it in their library. (Sorry, sweetie - pipe dreams of delusion and ridiculousness; you can't afford an attorney and I cleared it with mine; thus, no law suit. Better luck next time!).

Don't become preoccupied with your child's academic ability,
but instead, teach them to sit with those sitting alone.
Teach them to be kind. Teach them to offer help.
Teach them to be a friend to the lonely.
Teach them to encourage others.
Teach them to think about other people. Teach them to share.
Teach them to look for the good.
This is how they will change the world.
-Author Unknown

Major Depressive Disorder (Depression/MDD)

Major depressive disorder (MDD), also known simply as depression, is a mental disorder characterized by at least two weeks of low mood that is present across most situations. It is often accompanied by low self-esteem, loss of interest in normally enjoyable activities, low energy, and pain without a clear cause.

What was previously known as melancholia and is now known as clinical depression, major depression, or simply depression and commonly referred to as major depressive disorder by many Health care professionals, has a long history, with similar conditions being described at least as far back as classical times. The Persian and then the Muslim world developed ideas about melancholia during the Islamic Golden Age. Ishaq ibn Imran (d. 908) Major depressive disorder. (n.d.). Retrieved February 06, 2017, from https://

en.wikipedia.org/wiki/

1) Major_depressive_disorder combined the concepts of melancholia and phrenitis. The 11th-century Persian physician Avicenna described melancholia as a depressive type of mood disorder in which the person may become suspicious and develop certain types of phobias.

(2) Depression (major depression) Risk factors. (n.d.). Retrieved February 06, 2017, from http://www.mayoclinic.org/diseases-conditions/depression/basics/risk-factors/con-20032977

Depression Causes and Risks Factors

It's not known exactly what causes depression. As with many mental disorders, a variety of factors may be involved, such as:

Biological differences; people with depression appear to have physical changes in their brains. The significance of these changes is still uncertain, but may eventually help pinpoint causes.

Brain chemistry; neurotransmitters are naturally occurring brain chemicals that likely play a role in depression. Recent research indicates that changes in the function and effect of these neurotransmitters and how they interact with neurocircuits involved in maintaining mood stability may play a significant role in depression and its treatment.

Depression often begins in the teens, 20s or 30s, but it can happen at any age. More women are diagnosed with depression than are men, but this may be due in part because women are more likely to seek treatment. Factors that seem to increase the risk of developing or triggering depression include:

History of other mental health disorders, such as anxiety disorder, eating disorders or post-traumatic stress disorder.

Abuse of alcohol or illegal drugs.

Serious or chronic illness, including cancer, stroke, chronic pain or heart disease.

Certain medications, such as some high blood pressureself-critical or pessimistic medications or sleeping pills (talk to your doctor before stopping any medication).

Traumatic or stressful events, such as physical or sexual abuse, the death or loss of a loved one, a difficult relationship, or financial problems.

Childhood trauma or depression that started when you were a teen or child.

Blood relatives with a history of depression, bipolar disorder, alcoholism or suicide.

Being lesbian, gay, bisexual or transgender in an unsupportive situation.

Serious or chronic illness, including cancer, stroke, chronic pain or heart disease.

(2) Depression (major depression) Risk factors. (n.d.). Retrieved February 06, 2017, from http://www.mayoclinic.org/diseases-conditions/depression/basics/risk-factors/con-20032977

Depression Types

Depression (major depressive disorder or clinical depression) is a common but serious mood disorder. It causes severe symptoms that affect how you feel, think, and handle daily activities, such as sleeping, eating, or working. To be diagnosed with depression, the symptoms must be present for at least two weeks.

Some forms of depression are slightly different, or they may develop under unique circumstances, such as:

Psychotic depression; occurs when a person has severe depression plus some form of psychosis, such as having disturbing false fixed beliefs (delusions) or hearing or seeing upsetting things that others cannot hear or see (hallucinations). The psychotic symptoms typically have a depressive "theme," such as delusions of guilt, poverty, or illness.

Seasonal affective disorder; is characterized by the onset of depression during the winter months, when there is less natural sunlight. This depression generally lifts during spring and summer. Winter depression, typically accompanied by social withdrawal, increased sleep, and weight gain, predictably returns every year in seasonal affective disorder.

Bipolar disorder; is different from depression, but it is included in this list is because someone with bipolar disorder experiences episodes of extremely low moods that meet the criteria for major depression (called "bipolar depression"). But a person with bipolar disorder also experiences extreme high – euphoric or irritable – moods called "mania" or a less severe form called "hypomania."

Examples of other types of depressive disorders newly added to the diagnostic classification of DSM-5 include:
disruptive mood dysregulation disorder (diagnosed in children and adolescents) and premenstrual dysphoric disorder (PMDD).

Mental Health Information (n.d.). Retrieved February 06, 2017, from https://www.nimh.nih.gov/health/topics/depression/index.shtml

Depression Signs and Symptoms

Although depression may occur only one time during your life, usually people have multiple episodes of depression. During these episodes, symptoms occur most of the day, nearly every day and may include: Feelings of sadness, tearfulness, emptiness or hopelessness, angry outbursts, irritability or frustration, even over small matters. Loss of interest or pleasure in most or all normal activities, such as sex, hobbies or sports.

Sleep disturbances, including insomnia or sleeping too much. Tiredness and lack of energy, so even small tasks take extra effort. Changes in appetite — often reduced appetite and weight loss, but increased cravings for food and weight gain in some people.

Anxiety, agitation or restlessness.

Slowed thinking, speaking or body movements.

Feelings of worthlessness or guilt, fixating on past failures or blaming yourself for things that aren't your responsibility.

Trouble thinking, concentrating, making decisions and remembering things.

Frequent or recurrent thoughts of death, suicidal thoughts, suicide attempts or suicide.

Unexplained physical problems, such as back pain or headaches. For many people with depression, symptoms usually are severe enough to cause noticeable problems in day-to-day activities, such as work, school, social activities or relationships with others. Other people may feel generally miserable or unhappy without really knowing why.

Depression symptoms in children and teens:

Common signs and symptoms of depression in children and teenagers are similar to those of adults, but there can be some differences.

In younger children, symptoms of depression may include sadness, irritability, clinginess, worry, aches and pains, refusing to go to school, or being underweight.

In teens, symptoms may include sadness, irritability, feeling negative and worthless, anger, poor performance or poor attendance at school, feeling misunderstood and extremely sensitive, using drugs or alcohol, eating or sleeping too much, self-harm, loss of interest in normal activities, and avoidance of social interaction.

Children with attention-deficit/hyperactivity disorder (ADHD) can demonstrate irritability without sadness or loss of interest. However, major depression can occur with ADHD.

Depression symptoms in older adults

Depression is not a normal part of growing older, and it should never be taken lightly. Unfortunately, depression often goes undiagnosed and untreated in older adults, and they may feel reluctant to seek help. Symptoms of depression may be different or less obvious in older adults, such as:

Memory difficulties or personality changes.

Physical aches or pain.

Fatigue, loss of appetite, sleep problems, aches or loss of interest in sex— not caused by a medical condition or medication.

Often wanting to stay at home, rather than going out to socialize or doing new things.

Suicidal thinking or feelings, especially in older men.

When to see a doctor

If you feel depressed, make an appointment to see your doctor as soon as you can. If you're reluctant to seek treatment, talk to a friend or loved one, a health care professional, a faith leader, or someone else you trust.

When to get emergency help

If you think you may hurt yourself or attempt suicide, call 911 or your local emergency number immediately.

Also, consider these options if you're having suicidal thoughts:

Call your mental health specialist.

Call a suicide hot line number — in the U.S., call the National Suicide Prevention Lifeline at 1-800-273-TALK (1-800-273-8255). Use that same number and press "1" to reach the Veterans Crisis Line.

Seek help from your primary doctor or other health care provider.

Reach out to a close friend or loved one.

Contact a minister, spiritual leader or someone else in your faith community.

If a loved one or friend is in danger of attempting suicide or has made an attempt:
Make sure someone stays with that person
Call 911 or your local emergency number immediately! Or, if you can do so safely, take the person to the nearest hospital emergency room.

Happy Valentine's Day to the love of my life, my best friend, the glue that holds me together and attempts to keep me sane when I want to pull out my hair! Couldn't have survived these past 19 months without ya!

'Most of all, I miss my friend;
the one my heart and soul confided in, the one I felt the safest with,
the one who knew just what to say, to make me laugh again,
let the light back in,
I miss my friend.'
'I Miss My Friend' - Darryl Worley

cuz ya gotta have boots in Texas

On the 16th, I headed out to San Francisco to see our friends who live in Oakland. Homa picked me up at the airport; then we'd picked up Matt, from the school where he teaches, and head to Lake Tahoe for the four-day weekend. Tim was originally supposed to come along; but he got tied up with work, so I went alone. I have never been to Lake Tahoe and it was so beautiful! It snowed our first day there and a blizzard hit our last night there. We had a great time visiting, playing cards and jinga. I played craps for the first time and won!

Me and Dirk a.k.a Matt
Matt is 6'10 and looks exactly like Dirk
Nowitzki from the Dallas Mavericks, so of
course I call him Dirk and people always think
it's really him! He was surly on this trip, not
only refusing autographs, but photos as well. I
told him he'd end up on tabloid and give Dirk a
bad name for being rude to 'his fans' in Lake
Tahoe!!I It irks him when I play like he's Dirk in
public & people believe me!

The mind replays what the heart can't delete.

I'm a Daddy's girl. Always was. Always will be.

When I met my now-husband, Mitch, my dad took to him instantly. This was quite an accomplishment, given all former boyfriends had to proceed with caution — Dad could be a scary dude. Over time, their relationship grew into what could only be called father and son. The three of us were quite the trio! We loved life — together.

Unfortunately, that's not the story I'm here to tell.

I lost my father to suicide in March of 2014. I was in the third year of a clinical psychology doctoral program. However, no class, therapy session or research paper could have prepared me for this crushing blow. This was my best friend, my supporter, the coolest guy I know — my dad.

The first few weeks were a whirlwind in which Mitch and I were tasked with getting all of Dad's proverbial ducks in a row, and tying up the seemingly endless loose ends. Fortunately, through all of this, there was an overwhelming outpouring of love and support.

Friends and family members called, texted and emailed incessantly. There were cards, flowers, fruit baskets (and booze – folks definitely brought over booze). Groups of friends appeared for impromptu visits, and the attendance at the funeral service was staggering. Hundreds of people arrived to not only pay their respects, but to be there for us.

Then it all stopped.

No more phone calls. No more texts or emails. And definitely no more flowers or visits. What the hell? Mitch and I chalked it up to people being busy and having lives of their own. That's understandable. I mean, there was no way people could forget about us. We just lost our father to suicide; but over time it became apparent we weren't on the receiving end of peoples' forgetfulness.

Their memories were intact. It wasn't simply that folks were wrapped up in the day-to-day, focused on their own families and interests. The quiet took on a different feel. It seemed as though people were avoiding talking about our loss. The mention of Dad in conversation appeared to induce uneasy smiles, fidgeting or a swift change in subject. We were at a loss, and the silence was deafening.

So eventually I asked. I flat out asked a friend of 25 years why she hadn't been reaching out about how we are doing, or more importantly, why she rarely spoke of my dad. Her response was simple: "I don't know what to say."

Unfortunately, there is no script for this kind of thing. There was no right or wrong. I simply wanted to talk, reminisce, laugh, maybe even cry. Not all the time — just every once in a while.

Although I pride myself on being a tough cookie (some might say that "hard ass" is more appropriate), I wanted to know that support was there, should I need it. More importantly, I wanted the loss to be acknowledged. My friend also shared her feelings of anxiety about potentially causing me to have a bad day, or to think about the loss when I otherwise wouldn't have been. This is a kind sentiment, and one I have heard from numerous others over time. I also lost my older brother to suicide in 1996.

I was young-ish, which inspired my parents to lie for years about the true cause of death (I was told it was a car accident). More silence. So my response to all of you caring, protective types is this: Suicide loss survivors don't forget. The loss is, and will be, with me at all times. It is now an integral part of who I am. I mean, I'm not walking around sobbing, but the void is still there. And that's OK. Through my pursuit of psychology, and study of suicidology, I have gained liberal awareness of the prevalence of stigma. That little five-letter word is a bully, and is likely responsible for not only the silence Mitch and I experienced after the loss of my dad, but the silence subsequent my brother's passing, and in the lives of countless survivors of suicide loss. Unfortunately, stigmatization and negative attitudes towards mental illness remain prevalent in society. Suicide is prone to stigmatize both the deceased and loss survivors, often leading those left behind to experience rejection, shame and guilt.

Many don't realize stigma does not only manifest in the "typical" overt ways (intentionally hurtful comments, shunning of survivors, judgment of the deceased as weak or selfish), but also presents through more omitting behaviors (avoidance of conversation about the deceased, a lack of interest in the wellbeing of the survivor). Silence in a place where an individual expected support can be the most devastating. We are strong. However, survivors of suicide loss, especially family members, are at a particularly high risk for depression and co-morbid suicidal ideation and behaviors. Be mindful. It's time to fill the silence. Approximately 90 percent of those who die by suicide have a diagnosable mental illness at the time of their death. Suicide is not weak, selfish or the result of a character flaw — it is, for lack of a better explanation, a monstrous side-effect of an illness. It is not a wish to die, but the desire to end pain. Replace your judgment with compassion and understanding.

'You can't be brave if you've only had wonderful things happen to you.'– Mary Tyler Moore

Open your mind, your eyes and your mouth. Reach out to those left behind. Educate. Advocate. Eradicate stigma. Be the voice to end suicide. Remember, and speak of those lost fondly and often. Talk, reminisce, laugh, cry and heal. If you or someone you know needs help, visit our suicide prevention resources page.

If you need support right now, call the National Suicide Prevention Lifeline at 1-800-273-8255 or text "START" to 741-741.

On the 24th, I was interviewed live on the KTEN morning program!

"Our Year of First Without You" Attempting to End Suicide and Promote Organ Donation Awareness
Posted: Feb 24, 2017 10:46 AM CST
Whitewright mother, Bobbi Gilbert lost her teenage son almost two years ago to suicide. Since then, she's written a book called "Our Year of First Without You" A Journey Through Suicide and Organ Donation.
In the book Bobbi talks about what happened and how her son Pierce took his own life, as well as those who survived because of the donation of his organs. Now, she's hoping to raise awareness about organ donation and bring the stigma of talking about suicide to an end.
To buy the book visit: www.amazon.com/Our-Year-First-Without-You

Thank you Pierce for my sign today! luv ya better than Dr Pepper!

One organ donor can save
the lives of eight people.
Share this and share life.

'Mama, come here
approach, appear.
Dad, I know you're tryin,
to fight,
when you feel like flyin.
But if you love me, Don't let go.
Oh, oh⬛ .
If you love me, Don't let go.
Oh, o⬛ .h
Cuz I'm a little unsteady'
'Unsteady' – ⬛ Ambassadors

On my birthday, Josh & Michelle sent me presents and the boys made me homemade cards! Even though Josh and I haven't known each other for even half a year yet, they remember my birthday and sent gifts.

cards from my nephews in Chicago

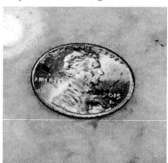

Thanks for the birthday present Pierce⊠

This year my birthday fell on Fat Tuesday; so our friend's, theStrippolli's, attended a wine dinner with us at our favorite restaurant in Sherman, Fullbellie's. It was a great meal and fun night!

'You all have concerns about the subject – FEAR, but a real man admits his fears ⊠ ..
-Gene Hackman's character ⊠head coach⊠in The Replacements

'If you're playing and you think everything is going fine; but then, 1 thing goes wrong, ⊠ then another. And you try to fight back, but the deeper you sink, until you can't move, can't breath, cuz you're in over your head – like ⊠uick sand.'
-⊠eona Reeves' character Shane in The Replacements

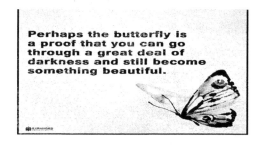

Perhaps the butterfly is a proof that you can go through a great deal of darkness and still become something beautiful.

March 2017

In honor of Pierce's favorite movie Forest Gump...one of his names was Forrest, after my grandfather, which I intended on calling him by....but after the movie came out, I knew he'd he teased if we called him that, so we chose to call him Pierce.

"Maw-maw always said dyin' was a part of life; I sure wish it wasn't"
- Forest Gump

I will always love and cherish this picture! Thank you Aimee Calvin Krisher for capturing this moment! This moment....soooooo shows Pierce's silly side. He was always willing to do whatever - if I asked. Morgan was always hesitant - not willing to let her guard down. P would just jump right in if I explained my reason for wanting it. He so adored his dad. He wanted nothing more than to grow up to be like him. Tim was for P, such a great example of what a man of God represented! P was lucky to have him as his dad for 17 years and 27 days!

'Our lives, are better left to chance,
I could have missed the pain,
but I'd had to miss, the dance.
'The Dance' – Garth Brooks

The beginning of March launches a very difficult 2- month period for me since Pierce's suicide. His birthday is March 24th & he would have been turning 19 this year. April 20th is the official date of death for him; but, I will always consider the 22nd to be the date of death since that's the day he was taken into surgery to harvest his organ's for donation. That's the day I felt him pass as he went up to Heaven while I sat in the hospital room with him, holding his hand.

Stopped by P's grave and saw these two baby bluebonnets popping up

I read an article about what you need to know if you're living with anxiety. It has some really good advice in it, so I thought I'd share it:

Last weekend, I went to a speed-dating event. Just walking up to the door made the hairs on the back of my neck stand up.

I like to think of myself as a social, outgoing person. But when it comes to anything related to dating, I can be painfully shy.

As I got closer to the building, I started to feel like there was some horrible, inaudible, invisible static in the air that only I could sense. To anyone else, I'm sure everything looked perfectly normal — the bar was nice, all the people I met were very lovely... but I couldn't help but feel that static playing across the back of my neck.

I was, in other words, anxious.

Everyone gets anxious sometimes, and that's OK.

In fact, anxiety is a normal and evolutionary biological response to stressful situations. Our brains are really good at linking bad experiences (like awkward dates) and stimuli together, mostly because it keeps us safe. If something bad happens and then you're in a similar situation in the future (like, say, having to talk to nearly 20 strangers in five-minute increments), your brain holds up big signs to help you remember to stay safe — signs like that prickling feeling on the back of my neck.

Other signs can be mental symptoms, like hypervigilance or intrusive thoughts, or physical ones, like a racing heartbeat or feeling nauseous or dizzy. **And these can sometimes be really, really hard to ignore.**

"[Anxiety is] a whole-body, a whole-mind, a whole-person experience," Dr. Michael Irvine told Upworthy.

Irvine is a clinical psychologist who knows a lot about anxiety. He's worked extensively with combat veterans experiencing post-traumatic stress disorder, a diagnosis that, at its heart, is about anxiety.

Irvine explained that **fighting off anxiety isn't as simple as just ignoring those anxious feelings.**

"It's not just battling your thoughts," said Irvine. "The work isn't just trying to convince yourself not to be scared. Anxiety is a reflex."

And anxiety doesn't just affect our bodies and minds; it can actually affect how we see the world every day.

An experiment from the Weizmann Institute of Science in Israel showed clearly that having anxiety can affect our ability to process sights and sounds.

Researchers from the lab set up the experiment by training volunteers with specific sounds. They taught them that some sounds had good outcomes (gaining money), and some had bad outcomes (losing money).

Then they started played the good and bad sounds, plus some benign and neutral ones, back to the volunteers. And what they found was fascinating: **The volunteers with anxiety were more likely to identify benign sounds as bad sounds, too, even though those sounds were neutral.**

Why? It wasn't a conscious decision. Instead, the anxious volunteers' brains had automatically overcompensated. In trying to keep them safe, their brains had changed the way they perceived all the sounds, not just the bad ones. This might sound like an odd scenario, but it helps to explain why the speed-dating event was so weird for me. To outsiders, the event looked like a couple dozen young people enjoying themselves. But **to my brain, through the filter of anxiety, the event was suddenly attached to bad dates of years past and uncomfortable social interactions.**

What might seem benign to everyone else actually looked much worse to me.

Sometimes, though, our brains take it too far.

Anxiety is normal — especially after a bad event — but, similar to how an overactive immune system can give us allergies, our brain's natural protective response can sometimes overcompensate. And when anxiety progresses to the point where it disrupts your everyday life, that's when it becomes what psychologists would call **an anxiety disorder.**

About 1 out of every 5 adults in the U.S. is affected by an anxiety disorder. Anxiety disorders come in a lot of different forms, too, ranging from social anxiety disorder to PTSD.

I don't have a diagnosed anxiety disorder, but for folks who do, the symptoms can be really paralyzing. Those intrusive thoughts and physical symptoms can keep people with anxiety disorders from leaving the house. The symptoms can make them struggle at work and seriously affect their quality of life. **The stigma of having an anxiety disorder can be just as tough as the symptoms, too.** Even though 1 in 5 people struggles with it, people who are living with anxiety disorders often feel like they should be able to fix themselves alone — to pull themselves up by their bootstraps. **In a 2007 survey, only 25% of people with mental health symptoms said they believed people would be sympathetic to their stories.**

But in reality, anxiety is nothing to be ashamed of; it's just your brain working extra hard. Plus, talking about your struggles and looking for treatment early are some of the best strategies for managing it.

"The earlier we intervene on the time line, the more likely an individual is to get a better outcome," said Irvine. **So biologically, it's not too weird to have a prickly-neck feeling or an upset stomach while meeting a bunch of strangers.** But when your brain is dealing with anxiety, especially an anxiety disorder, it actually functions differently. Things that might be benign suddenly seem scary. Meeting potential dates might make you really sweat. An overwhelming feeling of being unsettled might come over you just as you enter a new place that reminds you of an old place.

That is OK. Because even though we can't always control how our brains see the world, or what warnings signs they throw in our faces (needed or not), we've got nothing to be ashamed of when we start to feel anxious. And if you ever run into me at another speed-dating event, I hope you'll cut me some extra slack.

> *'All my burdens, are behind me. I have prayed, my last prayer.*
> *Don't cry, over my body, that ain't me, lying there.*
> *I am standing, on the mountain; I can hear, the angels song.*
> *I am reaching, over ⊠ordon, take my hand Lord, lead me home.'*
> *'High On The Mountain' – ⊠amey ⊠ohnson*

So these are my Tx. Country Peeps: Jack Ingram; Shooter Jeenings (Waylon Jennings son for your new-beebies); & Kevin from Two Tons of Steel!!!!! Cuz yeah, ya know that's how I roll!!!!! This year - gotta get one with me & Cody from Whiskey Myers in P's honor!

Jack Ingram

Shooter Jennings

Kevin Geil

On the 4th, my custom plates finally arrived! Of course they stand for Pierce Forest Gilbert, but Tim says P says they stand for Pierce F***in Gilbert!

I had a meeting with the new principal at Whitewright High School to clear the air about several misunderstandings over the past few months. Here is my post from that evening:

I am so incredibly thankful and humbled that Mr. Morrow, Principal at Whitewright High School, took time out of his incredibly busy schedule to meet with me today to clear the air on the past few month's missteps based on perception and hear-say.

He was very gracious in accepting my apology for what led me to use, what I considered accurate intel, in forming my opinions that led me to attack the district. The person who gave me the info, did so, without malice; based on her observations, and in defense of our son, for which, I will always be thankful to her. It was simply, a misunderstanding. Mr. Morrow was kind enough to accept my apology; knowing that since Pierce's decision, I am an advocate, & anytime I hear of any attempts to what I believe is to shut down promotion of suicide awareness, I will fight. We happily and respectfully came to a gentleman's agreement to check with each other first, after hearing statements made, to clarify, with the honor of always being forth-right.

In the end, I told him that I pray for him and do not envy him having to follow in the foot-steps of Mr. Kevin Weaver; who I consider, to be the best principal I have ever been graced to know. But, I feel this young man is up to the challenge and consider it a pleasure to know him.

That weekend, I was talking with my Chi-town nephews on the phone. Of course, Luke talked to me first and for the longest time. Then, he reluctantly gave it up to Connor, the 7-year-old. Connor and I spoke for about 20 minutes, then he asked, "Aunt Bobbi, how did Pierce die?"
I was shocked and totally caught off guard! How do you possibly answer a 7-year-old when they ask you that question? I immediately started crying; yet, desperately trying to hide that fact from him.
I said, "Oh sweetie, you're to young to know that." Connor: "No I'm not – I'm 7."
Me: "Sugar, can you please put your mom on the phone?" Connor: 'Why?"
Me: "Please babe, put your mom on the phone."
Michele: "Bobbi, I'm sorry. He was just innocently asking a question."

Me: "I know, but it hit me so out of the blue, so unexpectedly, that I didn't know what to say!" (I have since decided my reply will be either 'he died of a broken heart' or 'he wanted to go live with God and Jesus.'

On the 14th, Morgan left for Florida for spring break! So proud of her being brave enough to travel alone! Also proud she chose not to go to spring break in South Padre Island, knowing she wouldn't like to be in an all week long party fest.

fly away baby bird

On the 18th, we went to Love and War In Texas for Two Tons of Steels album release party. Their newest album is titled 'Gone' and Kevin Gill, lead singer, was kind enough to let me use the title track on my website – even before it was released! We had a great night with friends and family!

Me with Kevin before the show *Representing P w⊠his belt and buckle*

The gang with the band after the show!

What Bereaved Parents and Those Who Care for Them Need to Know
"It gets worse before it gets better." Those were the words the pastor offered to a newly bereaved couple whose daughter had died unexpectedly. And you should know that he is right.

Bereaved parents are stunned when four months, six month, nine months down the road they find their grief remains overwhelmingly raw. The shock has worn off.

Their hearts have been flayed open and the wound is still bleeding. It doesn't help that those outside the loss community expect healing to be happening when the magnitude of the loss is still seeping into the soul. The depth of loss has not been fully realized when the funeral is over.

No, in the weeks and months and years ahead bereaved parents are confronted with the realization that they didn't just lose their child but that they lost the hope, dreams and expectations they held forthat child as well. They lost their child's future, but they also lost their own future expectations (marriages and grand babies, to name a few) and they grieve for both what their child will never experience and what they themselves will miss out on. Frequently bereaved parents squelch their grief as they try to remain strong for their surviving children. They can't fall apart because they are so desperately needed by those too young to understand or to express their grief in healthy ways. That's one reason why the average length of time it takes for parents to work through the grief process averages five years or more – the longest bereavement period of any loss known to man.

My daughter's grief counselor told her that many teens don't grieve over lost siblings for four or five years. They experience delayed grief which I think results from trying to be strong for their parents. The entire home is in upheaval.

The sense of security that was taken for granted has been exposed for the fallacy that it is. Gone is the naïveté that we can protect those we love from harm. It's a frightening experience.

It's truly terrifying.

And parents and siblings are often left dealing with problems that arise in the wake of the death.

Financial pressure, legal issues, spiritual, emotional and health problems assault the family. Marriages and family relationships quake in the aftermath. While the outside world expects healing to begin, bereaved families are often sorting through compounding problems. They are reeling from the fallout and haven't really begun the healing process.

Bereaved parents and the outside world need to know and understand that grieving the loss of a son or daughter – regardless of their age – is the most devastating and destructive loss experience. Both the bereaved and those who care for them need to anticipate and make accommodations for a long and drawn out grieving process, because it definitely gets exponentially worse before it gets better.

grieve. Let go of the expected length of bereavement. Don't reduce grief to a simple bid for sympathy or pity. And be ever aware that for the grief-stricken feeling bad feels bad, but feeling minds of loss struggle to reconcile the conflicting messages received from the heart and mind. The solution is not as simple as mind over matter. People often ask me what to say or do for someone who is grieving. So many times I've heard others advise just be present and listen. Both those things are helpful but not necessarily healing. In my experience validating feelings is the single most healing thing you can provide the bereaved.

Grief, for a bereaved parent can be likened to a pressure sore, more commonly known as a bedsore. Pressure sores develop when an individual stays in one position for too long. Unlike other wounds, a pressure sore grows deeper instead of spreading wider as other wounds do. They can be deceptively dangerous because they rapidly eat through layers of flesh below the affected skin to the tendons and the bones beneath if not treated promptly. Treatment involves the painful scraping away of the dead tissue to reach the healthy tissue below. Ointments is applied, the wound is packed and covered and daily cleaning is required to prevent the wound from getting deeper.

Likewise, grief gets worse and deeper when exposed to the pressure of society to project a positive outlook or to work through their grief in the time frame others deem appropriate. Shaming and silencing the bereaved for failing to heal, wallowing in grief, or throwing a pity party deepens the wound by invalidating the worth of the loved one lost. Venting the negative feelings helps to clear away the infection but refusing to validate those feelings is tantamount to leaving the wound exposed to the dirt and debris floating in the air. The wound gets worse and healing takes longer as the grief-stricken seek the understanding of others.

Validation is the antibiotic ointment applied to promote healing. The presence of "safe friends" (those who don't criticize or try to fix the broken) is the packing and covering which provides a barrier between the open wound and the influences of the outside cleaning and disinfecting the wound. The wound may no longer be visible to the outside world but is quietly festering beneath the band aid that it covers. For the bereaved, be gentle and patient with yourself. You've been deeply wounded and deep wounds heal slowly. As the old song world. Frequent validation and affirmation keep the emotional wound clean providing an environment that encourages healing. The bad must be flushed out before the good can replace it. Unfinished grief occurs when we slap a band aid on without says, "The road is long with many a winding curve." Grief isn't supposed to feel good. It gets worse before it gets better; but, it gets better.

'Here I walk, in an empty shell.
Even though, it's hard to tell. This lonesome hand, it's taking its toll;
and I just don't know, how far it can go.
Well, come down and watch your first step.
Don't do anything you might regret. You're much to innocent to suffer.
It wasn't all sunny days, pickin' through my memories,
but the rain came down, and you covered me in velvet.
Oh, you covered me in velvet.
-'Velvet' Stoney LaRue

On the 22nd, this arrived. It's official! Morgan was accepted into the Phi Theta Kappa Honor Society! We're so proud of her!

March 22, 2017
Day 81 of 365.
God is saying to you today,
"Trust Me. I have you covered.
I know where you are,
and where you're going."
Those obstacles that look like
they're never going to change,
you better get ready: this is a new day.
God is breaking chains that have held
you back. You're going to see increase,
restoration, healing, and breakthroughs.

Luv this is meme is dated March 22nd. 22 - his number -
obviously a message for me!

On the 23rd, I had an early birthday celebration for Pierce's 19th!
With his favorite beverage of course! I went a day early because rain
was predicted on his birthday.
Sonia and I had plans to have a picnic with him on his birthday, but
when I woke up very late on the 24th (because I did not sleep much
the night before), I was not up for seeing anyone or leaving the
house, so she and Joe went instead.

March 22. 2017

I received this review of my book from a local father:
'This book acts as a guide by providing key information about what signs to look for▨what to do if you're dealing with a loved one who is suicidal▨and steps to take to prevent it and bring awareness! Highly recommend it to all parents, even if your child is not currently suffering, you never know when things might change. Know the facts and be prepared.'

It is such a huge honor to have people 'get' the intent of my book. It's not just about us, our life, or remembering Pierce. It's intended to be a guide, a resource of information, and hopefully a tool to spread awareness and save lives!

A friend of mine from the Lovejoy area asked me to come be a guest speaker for the PTA program in April. On the 28th, a friend posted this on her time line and tagged me in it: Just saw this in the school's newsletter...

PTSA Parent Workshop: April 5

One of the most difficult challenges of parenting is realizing you don't always know what children are thinking and feeling. You might even be aware suicide is the third leading cause of death in adolescents, but you can't imagine your child might become one of those statistics. When do normal ups and downs of adolescents become something to worry about? And if you are worried about it, what can you do?

Although adults don't often know about it, many of our kids experience symptoms of depression, think about suicide, make plans to die by suicide, and even make a suicide attempt each year.

The PTSA will host a parent prevention workshop. The guest speaker will be Bobbi Gilbert (former Lovejoy parent) whose own son committed suicide 23 months ago. The goal is to help parents equip themselves with signs to be aware of, and how we can help our children.

The first step is to learn about the factors that can put a teen at risk for suicide. The more you know, the better you'll be prepared for understanding what can put your child at risk.

Wednesday, April 5, 2017
7:00 PM
Lovejoy High School Library

'Ive got to walk away, while there's still hope;
learn to erase, the love I know,
and let you go.

'Cause what I thought was love, was only lies;
taking what you want, left me behind,
as my heart dies.

So here we are again; knowing this will never end,
so I must let go.
This is my last good-bye.
I'm leaving all the memories of you behind.
'My Last Good-bye' - Trading Yesterday

Morgan's best friend is pregnant and her water broke 14 weeks to early, so she is on permanent bed rest at Baylor Hospital. So, I went to see her. I haven't been able to step back into a hospital room since Pierce's the day he was taken into surgery for his organ's being harvested. But, I felt I really needed to go see her. Her fiancé met me downstairs to show me how to get to her room.

I walked into her room and my body immediately began shaking (the way I did for 6 months after P's passing). Cole said, "If your cold, I can get you a blanket." I had to explain to him that it was just my body's reaction to being back in a hospital room. She commented she was surprised I could even be there!

This was taken at my niece's wedding a few years ago. This is P with my Aunt Jerri and her daughter Emily. I love seeing photos of him with family and this was such a great night!

My post:
If Casper the Friendly Ghost a.k.a. Pierce, would stop making things disappear, that'd be great! (*I still cannot find my boots I bought in Fredricksburg several years ago!*)

A friend posted the following review of my book and I have chosen a selected sentence for discussion:
The blessing of Pierce's death is that he saved lives through organ donation.
Yes, a million times yes; but we still DO NOT HAVE OUR SON.
Our young son, who should be beginning the rest of his life!!
I recall one of the recipients, invited us to the one-year mark of their life-saving surgery party; yet, there was NO WAY I'd be celebrating that day!! I know the invitation was not, in any way shape or form, out of malice. Yet. while they are happy and celebrating their 2nd chance at life (which we are so happy and thankful for them); one must recall; their celebration, is our day of misery. The day he died. Yes, we're happy for their second chance at life; but, the bottom line is , we **DO NOT HAVE OUR SON!!!!!**
I will NEVER/EVER participate in any celebration on the date of the death of my child!
I get that this is such a total mix bag of tricks – we love them, glad to know them, happy they're alive; happy they now have aspects of him, etc. But, **WE DON'T HAVE HIM; OUR BOY**, our hot-headed teenager, our funny, sarcastic, fun-loving, stubborn, caring, loving, snarky 17-year old anymore. And, sadly, that's the bottom line.
We will FOREVER love his recipients and count them as family; yet, there will always be that.

A few months past this point, when Alicia, his kidney/pancreas was getting married, and Morgan found out our gift to them was paying for their photographer, she said, "Why do feel the need to continue to do anything for 'these people?' She so loves David Ray and Alicia, that her statement caught me off guard. In refection, it totally lends itself to her total distancing of herself from the loss of her brother – her best friend. She is now placing all of her anger, her rage, her hurt, over losing him, onto them; because, since her brother is dead, they are alive.

I continually pray she will somehow, someday, finally face and deal with the bottom line – her life-long best friend, the person she loved more than life itself, her person, the one she was not to go through life without – is gone. He's gone and not coming back; yet, watching over her from above.

April 2017

She is starting to talk about him a little more on occasion, which is good. I can sometimes mention him without her lashing out to me; so, little improvements are being made. Our relationship is mending and getting better every day.   One day while running errands, we had several moments where we discussed P and shared memories. While laughing, we both agreed it's amazing he left God's green earth without ever getting his butt kicked since he was so cocky and 10 feet tall and bullet proof!

Tim had to go get his driver license renewed. When the lady at the DPS asked if he would like to register as an organ donor, he said absolutely! She looked at him oddly and said, "Wow. We don't normally get that kind of reaction or enthusiasm when we ask that question." He replied, "Yeah, well my son saved five lives, so we're pretty big on the idea of it."

April 6th, I gave my speech to Lovjoy's PTA that evening. It was a small group, about 20 people, which I knew most of them, so it was a good first time out of the chute to get me feet wet. There were several students in attendance and I was glad to make my point to them that SUICIDE IS A PERMANENT SOLUTION TO A TEMPORARY PROBLEM!

At the end of my speech, I showed the MNHS PALS video and it had a huge impact on the crowd. There wasn't a dry eye after it aired.

This is my post from that evening:
Wow! Just Wow!
Incredible night speaking at my first gig and blessed our original stomping grounds held it!
THANK YOU LOVEJOY ISD for being brave and not turning your back on the subject of suicide!!!!!!! Thank you to my dear friend who brought this program to the parents of the district. Thank you to all the parents who took time out of their Wednesday evening to show up and learn about the warning signs and how to help those in need. Thank you to the parents who were aware enough to bring their children to the presentation.
As I said to them tonight, '**SUICIDE IS A PERMANENT SOLUTION TO A TEMPORARY PROBLEM!!!!!!!** #TeamPierce

Olivia, who went to Lovejoy with Morgan, posted the following:
Mental illness advocacy has always been something near and dear to my heart. Mental illnesses are just like any other disease and we shouldn't be afraid to speak up about it. Those who are suffering from these illnesses always remember you are not alone and don't be afraid to ask for help. "A semicolon is used when an author could've chosen to end their sentence, but chose not to. The author is you and the sentence is your life." #semicolonproject #mentalhealthawareness — at University Of Mississippi Oxford,MS

This was my reply to her post:

Thank you! When I showed your PALS video tonight after my speech, there wasn't a dry eye in the house! You did good girl! And the icing on the cake was it was presented at your previous district! I stood proud after the airing of the video to announce that you are doing fine and well at Ole Miss!

On the 12th, we started a new tradition @ P's grave borrowed from the Jewish faith. When people visit, they can mark a stone to leave there; that way, when we visit, we'll see that people have stopped by.

It has been meaningful in the months following this post, to stop by and see new stones being added. It's so comforting knowing that even two years later, people stop by to visit!

On the 8th, I placed the new velvet for P's grave....just in time for the 2 yr mark in a few weeks.

When I was visiting Heather at the hospital, she showed me the following article. It's a long read, but so mind blowing!

YOU WERE ON YOUR WAY HOME WHEN YOU DIED

You were on your way home when you died.
It was a car accident. Nothing particularly remarkable, but fatal nonetheless. You left behind a wife and two children. It was a painless death. The EMTs tried their best to save you, but to no avail. Your body was utterly shattered, you were better off, trust me. And that's when you met me.
"What.....what happened?" You asked me. "Where am I?"
"You died" I said mater-of-fact. No need mincing words. 'There was a... a truck and it was skidding'
"I.....I died?"
"Yep, I said.

But don't feel bad about it. Everyone dies."
You looked around. There was nothingness. "What is the place?" you asked. "Is this the afterlife?"
"More or less" I said.
"Are you God?" you asked.
"Yep," I replied. "I'm God."
"My kids......my wife," you said.

"What about them?"
"Will they be alright?"
"That's what I like to see," I said. "You just died and your main concern is for your family. That's good stuff right there."
You looked at me with fascination. To you, I didn't look like God. I just looked like some man. Or possibly a woman. Some vague authority figure, maybe. More of a grammar school teacher than the almighty.
"Don't worry," I said. "They'll be fine. Your kids will remember you as perfect in every way. They didn't have time to grow contempt for you. Your wife will carry on the outside, but will be secretly relieved. To be fair, your marriage was falling apart. If it's any consolation, she'll feel very guilty for feeling relieved."
"Oh," you said. "So what happens now? Do I go to Heaven or Hell or something?"
"Neither," I said. "You'll be reincarnated."
"Ah," you said. "So the Hindus were right?"
"All religions are right in their own way," I said. "Walk with me." You followed along as we strode through the void.
"Where are we going?"
"Nowhere in particular, I said. It's just nice to walk while we talk. You've been in a human for the last 48 years, so you haven't stretched out yet and felt the rest of your immense consciousness. If we hang out here for long enough, you'd start remembering everything. But, there's no point to doing that between each life."
"How many times have I been reincarnated, then?"
"Oh lots. Lots and lots. An in to lots of different lives," I said. "This time around, you'll be a Chinese peasant girl in 540 AD."
"Wait. What?!" you stammered. "You're sending me back in time?"
"Well, I guess technically. Time, as you know it, only exists in your universe. Things are different where I come from."
"Where you come from?" you said.

"Oh sure," I explained. "I come from somewhere. Somewhere else. And there are others like me. I know you'll want to know what it's like there, but honestly, you wouldn't understand."

"Oh," you said, a little let down. "But wait. If I get reincarnated to other places in time, I could have interacted with myself at some point."

"Sure. Happens all the time. And with both lives only aware of their own lifespan, you don't even know it's happening."

"So what's the point of it all?"

"Seriously?" I asked. "Seriously? You're asking me for the meaning of life? Isn't that a little stereotypical?"

"Well, it's a reasonable question," you persisted.

I looked you in the eye. "The meaning of life, the reason I made this whole universe, is for you to mature."

"You mean mankind? You want us to mature?"

"No, just you. I made this whole universe for you. With each new life you grow and mature and become a larger and greater intellect."

"Just me? What about everyone else?"

"There is no one else," I said. "In this universe, there's just you and me."

You stared blankly at me. "But all the people on earth…."

"All you. Different incarnations of you."

"Wait! I'm everyone?"

"Now you're getting it," I said, with a congratulatory slap on the back.

"I'm every human being who ever lived?"

"Or who will ever live, yes."

"I'm Abraham Lincoln?"

"I'm Hitler?" You said, appalled.

"And you're the millions he killed."

"I'm Jesus?""And you're everyone who followed him."

You fell silent.

"Every time you victimized someone," I said, "you were victimizing yourself. Every act of kindness you've done, you've done to yourself. Every happy and sad moment ever experienced by any human, was, or will be, experienced by you."

'What I wouldn't give to be sixteen, wild and free;
crusin' down main in my F-150;
with the windows down, bass way to loud,
from this burned out CD.
I'll be right where I wanna be, when I'm sixteen.'
'Sixteen' - Thomas Rhett

"Why?" you asked me. "Why do all this?"

"Because someday, you will become like me. Because that's what you are. You're one of my kind. You are my child."

"Whoa," you said, incredulous. "You mean I'm a god?"

"No. Not yet. You're a fetus. You're still growing. Once you've lived every human life throughout all time, you will have grown enough to be born."

"So the whole universe," you said, 'it's just…'"

"An egg." I answered. "Now it's time for you to move on to your next life."

And I sent you away.

New research shows that depression is an allergic reaction to inflammation

New research is revealing that many cases of depression are caused by an allergic reaction to inflammation. Tim de Chant of NOVA writes: "Inflammation is our immune system's natural response to injuries, infections, or foreign compounds. When triggered, the body pumps various cells and proteins to the site through the blood stream, including cytokines, a class of proteins that facilitate intercellular communication. It also happens that people suffering from depression are loaded with cytokines." Inflammation is caused by obesity, high sugar diets, high quantities of trans fats, unhealthy diets in general, and other causes.

By treating the inflammatory symptoms of depression — rather than the neurological ones — researchers and doctors are opening up an exciting new dimension in the fight against what has become a global epidemic. Caroline Williams of The Guardian writes: "The good news is that the few clinical trials done so far have found that adding anti-inflammatory medicines to antidepressants not only improves symptoms, it also increases the proportion of people who respond to treatment, although more trials will be needed to confirm this. There is also some evidence that omega 3 and curcumin, an extract of the spice turmeric, might have similar effects. Both are available over the counter and might be worth a try, although as an add-on to any prescribed treatment – there's definitely not enough evidence to use them as a replacement."

Eleanor Morgan of VICE adds: "Cytokines skyrocket during depressive episodes and, in those with bipolar disorder, halt in remission. The fact that 'normal,' healthy people can become temporarily anxious or depressed after receiving an inflammatory vaccine — like typhoid — lends further credence to the theory. There are even those who think we should re-brand depression altogether as an infectious disease … Carmine Pariante, a Kings College psychiatrist who is quoted in The Guardian report, says that we're between five and ten years away from a blood test that can measure levels of inflammation in depressed people. If both Pariante's estimate and the inflammation-depression theory are correct, we could potentially be just five years from an adequate 'cure' for depression."

You can read much more by visiting The Guardian, VICE, and NOVA. And to learn much more about how food and mood are powerfully connected, be sure to read this fascinating article on Kripalu.org. (Image courtesy of the American Heart Association).

TEACH YOUR KIDS THE WARNING SIGNS OF AN EMOTIONALLY ABUSIVE RELATIONSHIP:

At least he doesn☒ hit me.

That phrase, uttered by millions of women, has perpetuated an incomplete definition of the word "abusive." And it's not the only one. There are many skewed ideas about what constitutes an abusive relationship.

Not all abuse is physical. Not all abuse victims are women. Not all abusive relationships are romantic. Words and nonviolent actions can be just as damaging as slaps and punches — sometimes even more so.

We want our kids to make smart choices when it comes to relationships, but the unfortunate reality is that even healthy, smart kids can unwittingly form friendships or romantic interests with abusive people. Physical abuse is pretty straightforward; emotional abuse can be harder to spot. The sooner we teach kids to recognize the early warning signs that a potential friend or romantic partner might be an unhealthy choice, the better.

Here are some questions kids can ask themselves to help them recognize less obvious signs of abusive behavior:

Does the person seem unreasonably jealous?

Kids are just learning how to navigate social relationships in general, so some jealousy among friends is normal. But as kids get older, that kind of immature jealous reaction to friends hanging out with other people should wane.

Kids — and especially teens who are approaching the dating stage — should know that jealousy is not a healthy or flattering quality in a friend or potential love interest.

Does the person try to isolate you from others?

It's normal and healthy to have relationships with many people. If a friend or potential partner is trying to cut you off from others and keep you all to themselves, that's a red flag. If you find yourself losing friends or feeling guilty for spending time with other people, it's time to step back and reevaluate your relationship with that person.

Does the person make you feel bad about yourself?

You should never be in a relationship with a person who makes you feel down on yourself. Abusers can be master emotional manipulators. They may say or do cruel things, then say they're only joking. It's a classic pattern, making you feel bad and then making you feel guilty or stupid for feeling bad. Healthy relationships uplift you. Love doesn't demean or ridicule. Do they constantly call or text when you're not together? Puppy love can create a kind of "I can't stand being apart for five minutes" feeling, but there's a step beyond that which moves into obsession and control. If the person seems to be constantly checking in with you to see what you're doing or where you are or whom you're with, that's an unhealthy sign. Nobody needs a controlling friend or partner.

Do they "punish" you for not giving them enough of your time or attention? Abusers feel entitled to your time and attention and will make you pay in some way if they don't get it. They may turn cold and make you feel guilty. They may threaten to end your relationship. They may threaten to spread rumors about you. They may threaten to hurt you. They may even threaten to hurt themselves if you leave. Threats are red flags — always. Teaching our kids to treasure healthy relationships and steer clear of unhealthy ones is one of the most important life skills we can offer as parents. None of us want to imagine our kids being hurt by people who are supposed to care about them. If we teach our kids to be aware of warning signs, hopefully they won't find themselves in a relationship they have to fight their way out of — physically or emotionally.

Thanks to the people that walked into my life,
and made it better.
And thanks to the ones who walked out,
and made it amazing.

I feel very strongly about the above statement. After Pierce's suicide, several couples, we used to spend a lot of time with, stopped communicating with us. Even when I'd reach out to them, they could never get together because 'they were busy'. At first, I was confused and hurt by it; but, now I realize, it's a blessing. God removed them and replaced them with better, true friends.

Soooooo Excited!!!!!!! My book, is gaining ground internationally!!!!!!! We are in Canada, Mexico, Uganda, Scotland, Norway, France, and I am shipping one to Pakistan tomorrow!!!! Woo-Hoo for #TeamPierce

> PEACE I LEAVE WITH YOU;
> MY PEACE I GIVE YOU.
> I DO NOT GIVE TO YOU
> AS THE WORLD GIVES.
> DO NOT LET YOUR HEARTS
> BE TROUBLED AND
> DO NOT BE AFRAID.
> *John 14:27*

On the 12th, the TV show '13 Reasons Why' started. It's based off the book; which, is about a girl who commits suicide and leaves tapes behind for the people who lead to her choice. While I personally have not viewed it, I have seen numerous articles, reviews, post, etc. about it. Someone asked my opinion of it. For me, I feel it's necessary. It's at least getting suicide talked about and to the forefront; so, in my book, that's a good thing. However, I wish they had consulted mental health professionals before airing it; as it has now, been linked to two suicides of young girls who watched it.

> *'I've been talking to Jesus, but only when I needed to;*
> *there's lots to be forgiven, and it all comes back to you.*
> *...wanna hear your sweet voice calling, down the valley,*
> *through the pines, I need something to believe in, a little thirsty for the truth.*
> *I've been running short on faith, my faith runs back to you.*
> *'Back To You' - Bleu Edmondson*

taken on our cruise, his favorite trip and our last family trip

That evening, I took a new friend, LaKisha, to dinner. She and I became friends when her nephew told her about my book and she started following me on-line. I didn't realize it until that night, but her nephew, was in culinary arts class with Pierce; and, he is the one we gave the Mrs. Sadler Culinary Arts scholarship to!

She shared with me how difficult her life has been and how she has battled depression; but, if I can survive Pierce's suicide, she can survive anything too! She thanked me for saving her life! WOW! That's a lot to take in, but it was my goal from writing the book – to save at least one life!

Oh my gosh! One of the best written articles of grief paired with faith that I have EVER read! It speaks to me on volumes that have never been heard before!!!!!

Confused but Confident
Count it all joy, my brothers, when you meet trials of various kinds, for you know that the testing of your faith produces steadfastness. And let steadfastness have its full effect, that you may be perfect and complete, lacking in nothing.
James 1:2-4
I know that my God is good. I know that His plans are right and true. I know that all things work for His glory and my good.
But I am confused.
Is it ok to say that?

I trust God knows what He is doing and I trust that He has a plan … but it doesn't make any sense right now.

If mom was going to die, why not just have her on the bus two weeks ago? Why put mom through the pain of grieving the loss of Dad, just to have her join him 13 days later? Why put the four of us through planning a second funeral with the ink still wet on our thank you notes from the last one? And what about the kids? Mom and dad faithfully served for so many years in preteens and Awana. Why put all those kids through the pain of losing Dad … just to rip mom away two weeks later? Last night I was listening to a sermon from Grace about the stages of faith. He talked about the wall… and how believers will eventually be led into a dark night of the soul so that they can move from knowing about God to knowing God. He was referencing the verse in James that instructs us to count it all joy when we endure trials because we know that the testing of our faith is what perfects us for every good work.

The pastor pulled his illustration from David, who had everything stripped away and was a fugitive for over a decade before his eventual assent to the throne of Israel. He explained that God had to strip away everything from David so that David could find that God was all he needed. This is what prepared him to reign and made him the best king to ever rule over Israel. As I listened to the sermon, I recognized my own feeling of having everything stripped away from me to leave me with only God to cling to. When Cassie called and told me mom was dead, I had a strange mixture of emotions… sure I was in shock, sad, hurt, and brokenhearted. But the overwhelming emotion today has been confusion.

Maybe downright curiosity.

God, what are you up to?

What are you trying to build in me and what great work do you have for me to do that requires a test of such fire? David endured a decade without his status, wife, family, dignity, and home country because he was destined to rule Israel for 40 years and would be the king to deliver Israel from their enemies. David would make Israel great again and that is exactly what he did, by delivering them from oppression and turning the heart of the people back to God. In all this success, David remained humble because God had taught him that this could all be taken away in an instant.

I am not called to rule a country, conquer an invading force, or return a nation to the Lord. But clearly God has a plan for my life and that plan requires a character in me that must be refined through the fire of pain.

Just as Jonah had no right to complain about the loss of the vine, I cannot bemoan God the loss of such amazing parents. Many are never blessed with such a caliber of parents in the first place and I should count myself blessed to have had Murray and Dianne in my life.

Today was a day of tears, and there will no doubt be more to come in the weeks that follow. It was also a day filled with stressful decisions… adult decisions that I never expected to be making at this stage in my life.

First there will be the week of busyness. I will continue to wonder what God is up to and I will ask for wisdom as we work through the complex legal process to follow. I will write another obituary, we will process another cremation, and we will make another slide show. We will order another set of flowers and each of us will give another speech at another memorial.

Then there will be the week of stillness… the week where reality sets in because both of my parents are gone and my life will never be the same.

We will sell the properties and liquidate the estate and divide the inheritance and settle the details. Items will be stored, others sold, and still others tossed out as trash.

Eventually normalcy will return, work will resume, and days will begin to progress with some semblance of order. Somehow all the pieces of life will come back together to form a new picture, a new future, unlike anything I ever imagined.

My hope and prayer is that in a year when I look back on this unimaginable tragedy, I will say with confidence, that God has shaped me into a stronger woman and prepared me for His great work in my life. Life is hard. No one makes it out alive. I am glad for community and I am grateful for family.

Above anything else, though, I am glad to know with absolute confidence that my parents are both alive and I will see them again. Hopefully a long time from now… but I know, I will see them again.

Someday from now, from the other side of eternity, I know that I will look back on this time and see the hand of God. I will see how he had shaped myself and my siblings, from this experience, and I will trace His fingerprints in our lives, as we each go on to do amazing things.

A tear will form in the corner of my eye, and God will wipe it away; but the tears on that day, will be tears of joy and gratitude, that in the darkest nights and the hardest moments, God never left me alone.

And, more importantly, He did not allow any of the pain to go on in vein, because every bit of it will be redeemed, both in this life and the next.

But we do not want you to be uninformed, brothers, about those who are asleep, that you may not grieve as others do who have no hope.

For since we believe that Jesus died and rose again, even so, through Jesus, God will bring with him those who have fallen asleep.
1 Thessalonians 4:13-14

This memory popped up from 8 years ago

It's Pierce and Karli dancing at her birthday party. He was so nervous, especially meeting her parents! It's cute she had to take her shoes off since she was taller than him!

Easter was on Sunday and my sister-in-law shared this photo of Josh and the kids! It's one of my favorite pictures! I still can't get over how much Luke looks like Pierce!

As iron sharpens iron,
so one person sharpens another.
-Proverbs ⊠. 1⊠

My post mid-month:
This week will be an extremely difficult week for me.
Officially, Pierce's day death is the 20th at 3:17a.m.
But for me, it will always be on the 22nd, the day they took him to surgery to harvest his organs.
That's the day I felt him pass through me on his way to Heaven.
Please pray for us throughout the this long, difficult week.
As always, we NEVER could have made it through this without your love, thought, prayers, and support!! #TeamPierce

This is today's blog from my website:
"I wouldn't do that" -
I recall the first time she broke up with Pierce.
He came home bawling and ran upstairs. I went up and knocked on his door and he told me to leave him alone. After about 20 minutes, he texted me, asking me to come upstairs. As I reached the landing, I prayed to God to give me the right words to say to him. I went in and sat on the edge of his bed and he said to me, "why is she doing this? I haven't done anything wrong!" We talked for a long time and he finally calmed down. As I was leaving his room, I turned back and asked 'You're not thinking about hurting yourself are you?' (it seemed strange to ask him that because NEVER in a million years did I EVER think he would do that!) He replied, "No Mom, I would never do that to you and Dad."
As they say, famous last words.....

Girlfriend Charged for Boyfriend's Suicide:
"You Just Have to Do It"
Girlfriend, then 17, sent boyfriend (18) text messages instructing and encouraging him to take his own life in 2014.
Her attorneys argue the texts were free speech protected by the First Amendment and didn't cause the boyfriend to kill himself.
Conrad Roy, who was battling with depression, anxiety and suicidal thoughts, was seeking help but was instead encouraged by his narcissistic 18-year-old girlfriend Michelle Carter to finish the job. When Conrad started to worry about the consequences of his suicide, Michelle promised it was not a big deal. "Everyone will be sad for a while, but they will get over it and move on. They won't be stuck in the depression" she wrote.
CONRAD: How was your day?
CARTER: When are you doing it?
CONRAD: Since you don't get your snapchat anymore, I sent them to you.
CARTER: (Smiley face) My day was okay. How was yours?
CONRAD: Okay.
CARTER: Go somewhere you know you won't get caught. You can find a place. I know you can. Are you doing it now?
CONRAD: Yes.
CARTER: That's great. What did you do?
CONRAD: Ended up going to work for a little bit and then just looked stuff up.

Several times Conrad hesitated, screaming deep inside for help, but Michelle was determined to be a grieving girlfriend, getting all the attention she craved.

"Always smile and yeah, you have to just do it, suicide." Michelle wrote. When Conrad had doubts. "You have everything you need. There is no way you can fail. Tonight is the night. It's now or never."

The haunting messages Conrad and Michelle exchanged The morning of July 12, at 4: 19 AM

CARTER: When are you gonna do it? Stop ignoring the question.

CARTER: You can't think about it. You just have to do it. You said you were gonna do it. Like I don't get why you aren't.

CONRAD: I don't get it either. I don't know.

CARTER: So I guess you aren't gonna do it then. All that for nothing. I'm just confused. Like you were so ready and determined.

CONRAD: I am gonna eventually. I really don't know what I'm waiting for but I have everything lined up.

CARTER: No, you're not, Conrad. Last night was it. You kept pushing it off and you say you'll do it, but you never do. It's always gonna be that way if you don't take action. You're just making it harder on yourself by pushing it off. You just have to do it. Do you want to do it now?

CONRAD: Good. I'm gonna go back too sleep. Love you. I'll text you tomorrow.

CARTER: No. It's probably the best time now because everyone is sleeping. Just go somewhere in your truck and no one is really out there right now because it's an awkward time. If you don't do it now you're never gonna do it, and you can say you'll do it tomorrow, but you probably won't. Tonight? Love you.

CONRAD: Thank you.

CARTER: For what. Are you awake?

CONRAD: Yes.

CARTER: Are you gonna do it today?

CONRAD: Yes.

CARTER: Like in the day time?

CONRAD: Should I?

CARTER: Yeah, it's less suspicious. You won't think about it as much and you'll get it over with instead of wait until the night.

CONRAD: Yeah then I will. Like where? Like I could go in any enclosed area.

CARTER: Go in your truck and drive in a parking lot somewhere, to a park or something. Do it like early. Do it now, like early.

CONRAD: Didn't we say this was suspicious?

CARTER: No. I think night is more suspicious, a kid sitting in his car turning on the radio. Just do it. It wouldn't be suspicious and it won't take long.

CARTER: Okay.

CONRAD: I don't know why I'm like this.

CARTER: Sometimes things happen and we never have the answers why.

CONRAD: Like, why am I so hesitant lately. Like two weeks ago I was willing to try everything and now I'm worse, really bad, and I'm LOL not following through. It's eating me inside.

CARTER: You're so hesitant because you keeping over thinking it and keep pushing it off. You just need to do it, Conrad. The more you push it off, the more it will eat at you. You're ready and prepared. All you have to do is turn the generator on and you will be free and happy. No more pushing it off. No more waiting.

CONRAD: You're right.

CARTER: If you want it as bad as you say you do it's time to do it today.

CONRAD: Yup. No more waiting.

CARTER: Okay. I'm serious. Like you can't even wait 'till tonight. You have to do it when you get back from your walk.

CONRAD: Thank you.

CARTER: For what?

CONRAD: Still being here.

CARTER: I would never leave you. You're the love of my life, my boyfriend. You are my heart. I'd never leave you.

CONRAD: Aw.

CARTER: I love you.

CONRAD: Love you, too.

CARTER: Okay. So you gonna do it?

CONRAD: I guess.

CONRAD: Okay. I'm taking Holly for a walk.

CARTER: When will you be back from your walk?

CONRAD: Like, five minutes.

CARTER: Okay. So you gonna do it?

CONRAD: I guess.

CARTER: Well, I want you to be ready and sure. What does that mean?

CONRAD: I don't know. I'm freaking out again. I'm over thinking.

CARTER: I thought you wanted to do this. This time is right and you're ready. You just need to do it. You can't keep living this way. You just need to do it like you did the last time and not think about it and just do it, babe. You can't keep doing this every day.

CONRAD: I do want to but I'm like freaking for my family I guess. I don't know.

CARTER: Conrad, I told you I'll take care of them. Everyone will take care of them to make sure they won't be alone and people will help them get through it. We talked about this and they will be okay and accept it. People who commit suicide don't think this much. They just could do it.

CONRAD: I know. I know. LOL. Thinking just drives me more crazy.

CARTER: You just need to do it, Conrad, or I'm gonna get you help. You can't keep doing this everyday.

CONRAD: Okay. I'm gonna do it today.

CARTER: You promise?

CONRAD: I promise, babe. I have to now.

CARTER: Like right now?

CONRAD: Where do I go?

CARTER: And you can't break a promise. And just go in a quiet parking lot or something.

CONRAD: Okay.

CARTER: Go somewhere you know you won't get caught. You can find a place. I now you can. Are you doing it now?

Later that afternoon, the conversation continued.

CONRAD: I'm determined.

CARTER: I'm happy to hear that.

CONRAD: I'm ready.

CARTER: Good because it's time, babe. You know that. When you get back from the beach you've gotta go do it. You're ready. You're determined. It's the best time to do it.

CONRAD: Okay, I will.

CARTER: Are you back?

CONRAD: No more thinking.

CARTER: Yes. No more thinking. You need to just do it. No more waiting.

CONRAD: On way back. I know where to go now.

CARTER: Where?

CONRAD: A parking lot. There is going to be no cars there at 9:00. So that's when I'll be found.

CARTER: Okay, perfect. When will you be home?

CONRAD: Ten minutes. Ha ha, that's perfect.

CARTER: Okay. And, well, yeah, I don't know.

CONRAD: Like, I don't want to kill anyone else with me.

CARTER: You won't.

CONRAD: When they open the door they won't know it's odorless and colorless.

CARTER: You're over thinking. They will see the generator and realize you breathed in CO too.

CONRAD: So should I keep it in the back seat or front?

CARTER: In the front. You could write on a piece of paper and tape it on saying carbon monoxide or something if you're scared.

CONRAD: I was thinking that but someone might see it before it actually happens.

CARTER: Well, wait, the generator is gonna be on because you'll be passed out, so they'll know you used carbon monoxide. Dead. It's not loud is it?

CONRAD: Not really, LMAO.

CARTER: Okay, good. Are you gonna do it now?

5:08 PM, Conrad returned from the beach and wanted to back out.

CONRAD: I'm home.

CARTER: Okay.

CONRAD: Ah.

CARTER: What?

CONRAD: I don't know. I'm stressing.

CARTER: You're fine. It's gonna be okay. You just gotta do it, babe. You can't think about it.

CONRAD: Okay. Okay. I got this.

CARTER: Yes, you do. I believe in you. Did you delete the messages?

CONRAD: Yes. But you're going to keep messaging me.

CARTER: I will until you turn on the generator.

CONRAD: Okay. Well, I'm bringing my sisters for ice cream.

CARTER: So will you do it when you get back?

CONRAD: Yup, I'll go right there.

CARTER: Okay.

CONRAD: Love you.

CARTER: I love so much.

CONRAD: (Smiley face).
CARTER: 33.
CONRAD: Ha ha. What are you doing?
CARTER: Nothing really. Just resting.
CONRAD: Okay. Ha, ha I'm procrastinating.
CARTER: Yeah, ha ha, I know. Are you back?
CONRAD: Yup.
CARTER: So it's time?
CONRAD: Oh, it's been time.
CARTER: Are you gonna do it now?
CONRAD: I just don't know how to leave them, you know.
CARTER: Say you're gonna go the store or something. CONRAD:
Like, I want them to know that I love them. CARTER: They know.
That's one thing they definitely know. You're over thinking.
CONRAD: I know I'm over thinking. I've been over thinking for a
while now. CARTER: I know. You just have to do it like you said.
Are you gonna do it now?
CONRAD: I still haven't left yet, ha ha.
CARTER: Why?
CONRAD: Leaving now.
CARTER: Okay. You can do this.
CONRAD: Okay. I'm almost there.

6:25 PM, the last message was sent.
After the exchange of these messages, Michelle left her house and
talked with Conrad for 43 minutes. According to the court
documents, at some point during that call, Conrad got out of the car
because he got scared, but Michelle told him to get back in. His body
was found in his pickup truck after his parents reported him missing.
On the day of Conrad's murder, Michelle was already seeking
attention on Twitter:
"Such a beautiful soul gone too soon." A little later she added: "I'll
always remember your bright light and smile. You'll forever be in my
heart, I love you Conrad." She even organized a suicide prevention
fund raiser in his name. – Fox News

I AM SO GLAD TO SEE HER GO TO TRAIL!!!!!! People have to learn that there are consequences for your actions. When I posted about this, someone commented that 'she didn't make him do it! She didn't pull the trigger." Yes, but she led to it and thus is being charged, as she should be!

Rape

If rape was about how revealing their clothes were, rape rates would quadruple during the summer.

But they don't.

If rape was about how much sex someone's had in the past, then virgins wouldn't get raped.

But they do.

If rape was about how attractive a person was by conventional standards, then only thin, white, abled people would get raped.

But they don't.

If rape was about how much they drank, then sober people wouldn't get raped.

But they do.

Rape is not the victims fault.

I feel strongly on this subject! Rape is a violent crime and in no way, shape, or form should the victim EVER be blamed! You wouldn't blame the deceased person from a drunk driving wreck for being hit by the drunk driver, so why would anyone ever blame a rape victim for their rape?

On the 19th, we were at the N. Texas Crime Commission luncheon w/ Sen. Cornyn. Our friend sits on the board and invited us to the luncheon. It was a great event and hearing Sen. Cornyn speak was fascinating! I never knew all about his career. He has accomplished so much and is a staunch supporter of law enforcement!

TBT to P's first year of LaX for Lovejoy

My post from the 20th:

This book is dedicated to my son,
Bobby Pierce Forest Gilbert,
who I was blessed to have in my life
for 17 years and 27 days.
I miss your smile, your laugh, your hugs,
your voice, and your 'I love you' before bed every night.
I will always love you better than Dr Pepper!

For:
My Loving, Supportive Husband Tim (who is my rock) –
I couldn't have survived this journey without you.

My daughter Morgan –
Who's love, strength, & hope for the future continues to amaze me.

Our family and friends –
We've held it together with duct tape, tissues and your prayers.

To God:
YOU ARE ALWAYS GOOD!
Thank you for your blessings & holding us tight in your loving arms through all of this.

some names have been changed

"Our Year of First Without You" 'A journey through suicide and organ donation'

April 20, 2015

5:55 a.m.

I think I see flashing lights through my still closed eyes. While in bed, I wonder why would a fire truck be here when the house doesn't smell like it's on fire? Then, it dawned on me; open your eyes, something is wrong.

I looked out my window to see a Sheriff's car with flashing lights on. I quickly dress and went downstairs to find the Sheriff on our porch. I couldn't for the life of me figure out why he'd be here.

I opened the door and he asked, "Are you Mrs. Gilbert?'

Yes.

"May I come in?"

Yes.

"Is Mr. Gilbert here?"

Yes, but he's asleep, what is this about?

"Ma'am, the Collin County Sheriff asked me to contact you." That's when I knew.

That's when our year of first started without you.

Of course, you woke me up
at 3:17 a.m.
Miss ya Pierce

I cried when I opened it! I love it!

My friend Amy posted this on the 20th and tagged me in it:

I cannot imagine the grief and sorrow carried by a family that loses a child. God is good. He is faithful...He is the only one who can heal our brokenness. I am so thankful to have the honor of praying over & alongside these 2 families. Please pray for the Gilberts as they honor the memory of Pierce and continue to carry his story with this 2nd yr.
Honor sweet Nancy Jane. It was wonderful seeing former students☒parents from our ☒th grade ☒ C class at visitation tonight. I pray for all the families attending her funeral tomorrow...for travel mercies, strength of spirit, and a stillness that transcends any understanding.

It broke my heart learning that sweet girl, who was a student at UT, took her life and now her family would be walking our same path. Sending lots of prayers their way.

'I had a dream about a burning house.
You were stuck inside, I couldn't get you out.
Laid beside you and I pulled you close, And the two of us went up in smoke. Love
isn't all that it seems, I did you wrong.
I'll stay here with you, 'til this dream is gone.
I've been sleep walking, been wondering all night;
Trying to take what's lost and broke, and make it right.
I've been sleep walking, too close to the fire;
But it's the only place I can hold you tight,
In this burning house'
'Burning House' – Cam

'Oh misty eye of the mountain below,
keep careful watch of my brothers soul,
and should the sky be filled with fire and smoke,
keep watch over Durin's son.'
If this is to end in fire, then we should all burn together. Watch the flames climb,
high into the night calling out father, oh, sent by and
we will watch the flames burn over and over, the mountain side.
And if we should all die tonight, then we should all die together.
Raise a glass of wine, for the last time, crying out father oh,
prepare as we will, watching the flames burn over and
over the mountain side, desolation comes upon the sky.
⊠ ow I see fire, inside the mountain;
I see fire, burning the trees. And I see fire, hollowing the souls.'
'I See Fire' – Ed Sheeren

Gee⊠I wonder where he got it from⊠

Great article:
"Chronic anxiety is a state more undesirable than any other, and we will try almost any maneuver to eliminate it," wrote Robert Robert E. Neale in The Art of Dying.

Anxiety is, indeed, a miserable affliction. However, it also lives in some of the most wonderful people in our world.

Anxiety Often Comes Hand-In-Hand With A High Iq, A Sensitive Soul, A Creative Nature, A Drive For Achievement, And The Simple Inclination To Care Too Much.

It's no wonder people often find themselves falling for the anxious.

Here Are 16 Things You Should Expect When Your Loved One Has Anxiety:

1.　　Expect firm boundaries.

Sometimes anxious people – and especially anxious introverts – simply need to be alone.

2.　　Expect to be appreciated for the little things.

We notice everything, and we are grateful for even the smallest of gestures.

3.　　Expect our bond to run deep and grow quickly.

Once you are in our inner circle, you are in for life.

4.　　Expect to be the one responsible for making plans.

Having too many choices can stress us out.

5.　　Expect to learn to listen, rather than give advice.

When we are anxious, we need to let it out. It's therapeutic.

6.　　Expect to endure hundreds of new attempts at anxiety management techniques.

Essential oils, adult coloring books, acupuncture…we'll try it all.

7.　　Expect to give reassurance more than you'd like to.

Tell us we're safe. Tell us we're loved. Tell us it'll all be okay.

8.　　Expect reason to be powerless against anxiety.

This is true for even the most logical of anxious people.

9.　　Expect to learn some deep breathing exercises.

Walk your partner through them in times of trouble. These are amazingly effective.

10.　　Expect to communicate honestly.

Your partner will sense if you are holding back. This will add to their anxiety.

11.　　· Expect some weird sleep patterns. Anxiety often goes hand in hand with insomnia and other sleep disorders.

12.　　Expect lots of lists and itineraries.

Preparation helps to soothe us. Please don't try to stray from the plan.

13.　　Expect to provide stability rather than drama.

We don't like to do the on-and-off thing. We need a partner we can depend on. We thrive on this.

14.　　Expect to encounter problems that you can't solve for us. Learn to be okay with that.

15.   Expect to encourage your partner to engage in self-care. Explain that it's not the same thing as being lazy or self-indulgent. Health is just as important as accomplishments.

16.   Expect to make your own self-care a priority.

Your well-being is important, too.

"Don't worry if people think you're crazy. You are crazy. You have that kind of intoxicating insanity that lets other people dream outside of the lines and become who they're destined to be," wrote Jennifer Elisabeth. Your partner's anxiety may seem insane to you at times. However, this is only one part of their being. If the rest of them is worth it, learn to love your partner as a whole. Get lost in their madness. Learn to love one another completely, strengths, afflictions, and all.

This was taken at the Magic Time Machine in Addison. Pierce harassed the wait staff. To this day, us and the Griffin's, laugh about it!

13 Reasons Why NOT

I'm sure you've heard of the hit series Thirteen Reasons Why that recently made its debut on Netflix.

If you haven't, it was based off a novel and has caused an uproar on social media and spiked many tough conversations. It's the story of a high school student, Hannah Baker, who takes her own life in the midst of suffering. Before she does so, she records herself on thirteen different tapes explaining the thirteen reasons of what drove her to end her life.

These tapes are dedicated to different incidences and different people who drove her to the end of herself. Hannah intends for each single one of these people to get the tapes to hear what they did.

Hannah Baker was the new girl, moved from far away and much like today's society, attended a high school that was full of hurt people and hurtful people. Rumors were spread, pictures were sent, words were said, whispers were heard, people were betrayed, and friends were lost.

She decided she couldn't take it anymore; the rumors.

The bullying.

The loneliness.

The betrayal.

The whispers.

While watching this, my heart was broken over the reality and rawness of the story that unfolded. Although this series focused on suicide, it also spoke to many other issues; drug abuse, alcohol abuse, sexual abuse and violence, domestic abuse, rape, and bullying.

These issues are SO REAL.

As a high school student in the public-school system, I am sure of one thing, this story isn't just cinematic; **this story happens EVERY SINGLE DAY. It is happening.**

It might be happening in your own life right now, or in your friends, maybe even your own child.

While this series gave you Thirteen Reasons Why Hannah Baker took her own life, I am going to give you Thirteen Reasons Why Not.

THIRTEEN REASONS WHY YOU SHOULDN'T

1) You are fearfully and wonderfully made. (Psalms 139:14)
2) You are WORTHY.
3) You are made in HIS IMAGE.
4) Your body is a temple (1 Corinthians 6:19-20)
5) Your body is NOT YOUR OWN. It belongs to Jesus.
6) You are MORE; More than the whispers, rumors, and loneliness.
7) Death has already BEEN DEFEATED; whatever you are fighting, Jesus already died for it.
8) YOU HAVE A PURPOSE.
9) Ultimately, you aren't in control, GOD IS.
10) Our God is BIGGER.
11) You can't give victory to the enemy. Those lies you hear, are solely of the enemy. Don't let him win.

12)   You aren't alone.
13)   God's plans for you are PROSPEROUS. It's not cliche', it's the
truth.
If you are considering self-harm or suicide, or are a victim of any of the
issues mentioned, I assure you, you aren't alone and getting help is crucial.
You are worth so much more than the whispers. Your life is precious.
In Christ, Lauren Faith

My post from the 24th:

Proud to announce tha I will begin writing my ⊠nd book⊠It's a continuation of my first, titled ';Living Without You.' So many have mentioned to me that there needs to be a ⊠nd book because so much has happened since our year of first without P.

We attended the 10th anniversary party @ Rick's Chophouse in old
downtown McKinney. It was a charity event and it raised over
$200k for numerous local charities!

An article published by Children's Medical Center:

Talking with your child about suicide

Learn the warning signs and how to start the conversation.

Suicide is the second leading cause of death among adolescents and young adults, according to the CDC Most suicide attempts in children and adolescents occur in the midst of depression or other mood disorders. Nearly one in five high schoolers have seriously considered suicide within the past 12 months, and about 8⊠ have made an attempt. Many do not want to die, but they feel ambivalent (i.e., have mixed feelings) about life and simply want to end emotional or physical pain.

Suicide is 100% preventable and there are effective treatments to help.

Dr. Nicholas J. Westers, a clinical psychologist at Children's Health , offers the following advice for parents.

Signs of depression and suicidal thoughts

Depression is more than just feeling blue or down in the dumps for a day or two. Instead, it is a change in usual behavior that lasts for several weeks. Signs of depression that can be warning signs of suicide in children and teens include:

Feeling persistently sad or blue

Becoming much more irritable or

suddenly getting into trouble a lot

Failing to engage in previously pleasurable activities or interactions with friends

Having a marked deterioration in school or home functioning Reporting persistent physical complaints and/or making many visits to school nurses

Talking about suicide or being "better off dead"

What can you do as a parent?

Look for everyday opportunities to bring up the conversation with your teen.

Was there a suicide covered by the news? Is your child's school implementing a suicide prevention program?

Is there a new television show depicting a suicide? Did you come across some new information or statistics about suicide?

Consider these conversation starters:

"I read a post on-line about how parents should talk to their children about suicide…"

"I was reading that youth suicide has been increasing…"

"I heard about a new TV show/movie that talks about suicide…"

"I see your school is having a program for teachers/students on bullying and suicide prevention…"

Ask your child if he or she has ever thought of suicide.

Some parents believe asking their child or others if they have ever thought about suicide will put the idea in their mind or make them more suicidal. It will not. In fact, many people who have been thinking of suicide feel relieved to talk about it, and research suggests that asking about it may make them less likely to consider it.

Consider these conversation questions:

"What do you think about suicide?"

"It sounds like a lot of young people have thought about suicide at some point. Do you know if any of your friends have?"

"Has this been something that's ever crossed your mind?"

Prepare yourself to respond calmly and nonjudgmentally, regardless of your child's response. Ask yourself what assumptions and beliefs you have about suicide and mental illness. Children often base their own assumptions about mental health and suicide on their parents' assumptions. An empathic and validating response from you could be the difference between suffering alone and seeking help if they experience depression or suicidal thoughts now or in the future.

Listen well to your child's response. This means refraining from providing immediate advice, but first asking clarification questions and reflecting back to your child what you are hearing. However, it is OK to be honest and express your concern.

Consider these responses after you listen well:

"It's really hard for me to hear that you've thought of ending your life, but I'm here for you and we'll get through this together."

"No matter what mistakes you might make in life, or what grades you get, your life is more important. Feelings come and go, but death is permanent. It's OK to feel guilt or sadness, but please let me know right away if you ever have thoughts of ending your life. We'll get through this together."

Seek professional help for yourself if needed.

Suicidal thoughts often occur in the context of a mental health disorder like depression or anxiety. And they do not go away on their own. Contact a mental health professional to discuss treatment options (e.g., psychologist or counselor for therapy, psychiatrist for medication).

It can be difficult to learn that your child is struggling. Family support is very important. Research shows that taking care of your own mental and emotional health as a parent can help your child recover from their own depression.

Learn more about Children's Health services for mood disorders such as depression in children and adolescents.

Additionally, the ⊠ational Suicide Prevention Lifeline
⊠1-800-⊠⊠3-8⊠55⊠is available ⊠4⊠⊠. You'll also find helpful information at
Suicide Prevention Resource Center and Suicide Awareness Voices of
Education ⊠SAVE⊠

I am so glad to see more focus being placed on suicide in relation to
our children! More centers need to be available to accept our kids and
recently, I've seen several private one's open in the Metroplex area of
N. Tx. In Grayson County, the current mental health center is going to
open a wing for children and youth, but it will only have 12 beds;
which will fill up quickly.

Moving on:
I never thought I'd ever consider moving from our ranch...unless it was
moving to the beach as a retirement home. But, within the last week,
the idea of selling our ranch and moving has come up. We've discussed
the house we thought about building here vs. the one we did. We've
talked about what changes we'd make to it, etc.

'Spent some time to count the reasons;
loss and pain, the changing seasons;
no one leaves an answer for you there;
it's just ⊠uestions ya never saw coming;
I never wanted to leave this town;
⊠ o, you never saw it coming'
'Texas' – Band of Heathen's

I never thought, after Pierce, I'd ever want to leave here; for, he loved it so, this is our last home with him, etc. But, you then think, maybe a change would be good for us. Maybe, building a new home, picking out new things for the home, etc would be good for us. After all, no matter where we go, I know Casper, our friendly ghost, will go with us. But tonight, Tim said to me, 'what's going on with you? Why this sudden urge to move?' I had to take a long hard evaluation of why and the conclusion was....bottom line, I miss him. As Tim said, 'Moving isn't going to change that.' Sigh........

BE STRONG BECAUSE IT WILL GET BETTER. IT MAY BE STORMY NOW BUT IT CAN'T RAIN FOREVER.

A friend posted this and tagged me in it:
This has got to be the most moving song and video I have ever experienced. Watch until the end. Listen intently. You will be moved. #changedirection. Bobbi Danice Morgan Gilbert what do you know about www.changedirection.org
(the song : *Chris Stapleton* *Fire Away*)

I booked Morgan's flight for a mission trip to Belize this summer! She has wanted to go to an impoverished area to teach the kids about nutrition; so when I saw that Olivia was going on one, I found out there was space available. We actually have another motive for sending her as well; since Pierce's death, she has said she doesn't believe in God anymore (her being angry at him over Pierce dying); so, we feel it'll be good for her to go with a church group and serve and hopefully she'll see God in the children's faces!

MAY 2017

For parents who lose a child to suicide and don't know why, it literally breaks my heart. I am thankful we know what led to Pierce's choice to take his life in his ex-girlfriend's yard in the early morning hours of April 20th 2015. The not knowing, racking my brain to figure it out, would literally drive me insane! I'm thankful for the kind note that he left for us, giving us additional insight. I'm thankful we knew he had been struggling and got him help. If he had done this 3 weeks prior to getting help, I would not be able to forgive myself. But, I know we did all we could to help him. I will forever be grateful for the last 2 weeks; prior to his death, when we saw the old, happy version of Pierce before she ever came into his life. Parents: if you see your child struggling, get them help - even if they claim 'they're fine' 'nothing is wrong' etc.

FOR THE KID WHO DOESN'T GET THE AWARD

The end of another school year is approaching, which means it's time for teachers to figure grades and determine which names will be recognized during the academic banquets and who will be awarded the gold medals for achievement.

These students are deserving of their honors. They read the novel instead of the online summary.

They memorize the math formulas. They understand science concepts such as the survival of the fittest.

But these academic heroes are just a small percentage of the student population who achieve amazing things in an average 180-day school year. And there are awards for students like these.

But in my 23 years of teaching, I've learned there are other students whose achievements are just as amazing…maybe even miraculous…but they are never recognized because we don't give awards to students like them.

So today I want to recognize them—the students who have sat in my classroom and others like mine—who approach those 180 days one day at a time because survival is the only concept they understand, and that's how they get through the 16,380 hours from kindergarten to graduation. Today I give the gold medal to these students:

The boy who works harder than the valedictorian of his class—but who will never get higher than a C;

The girl who knows all the answers but is paralyzed by shyness and cannot raise her hand;

The boy who just doesn't fit in, who tries but can't figure out why the other kids call him a freak;

The invisible girl whose day will end without one person speaking to her, including the teachers because they have 48 minutes to teach 32 students;

The boy who stifles his dream of going to college because he comes from a working family who has different plans for him; The girl who didn't finish her homework again—because she closed at McDonald's again—so she can pay the electric bill or buy groceries so her little brother can eat; the boy who is raised by loving grandparents but who needs me to be more of a mom than a teacher;

The girl who lived alone for three months, who had no idea where her mom was or if she was coming back;

The boy who discovers the constant fighting between his parents is over… and so is his family…and somehow he believes it's his fault;

The girl who cries herself to sleep because there's a man in her home she doesn't know, just like the one she didn't know last week, or the week before;

The boy who was unaware of his father's illegal activity, who shook in terror the night before when a task force swarmed his home and took away his hero in handcuffs;

The girl whose eyes hold dark secrets that cast shadows across her face, whose long sleeves cover the scars of her emotional pain, who struggles to control the anxiety boiling inside her—but sometimes fails;

The boy who sends me a message from jail and asks if I will send him some books to read;

The girl who watches through the keyhole in the bathroom door as her mother shoots up, even though she promised she'd stop;

And the girl who checks into rehab for the third time since freshman year and tells me, "Mrs. Sargent, this time I'm going to make it." (I couldn't force myself to attend her funeral.)

Each of these scenarios represents actual experiences, not just of one student but of many teens who have shared similar challenges in my classroom since August 1994. We don't give awards to students like these. There's no test to measure the thing inside them that sits there while I insist they learn to evaluate credible sources or analyze poetry or read Shakespeare. In school there's not a percentage to assign for "survival," so we can't record it in the grade book and declare a winner. But these students—they are heroes. And today…I give them the gold medal.

-Karen Sargent

On the 5th, Morgan attended a concert with her friend Madi in Dallas at Fair Park. For those of you unfamiliar with the Fair Park area of Dallas, it is one of the roughest neighborhoods in Dallas; but, that is where the State Fair is held every fall and during other times of the year, there are concerts held there. Madi got drunk and kept disappearing on Morgan and when Morgan finally found her, she said she had called her husband to come get her. Morgan called me to come get her and I could tell she was scared and frightened. I told her to catch an Uber ride and I'd meet her half way.

We always have said to our kids, call anytime and we'll come get you, no questions asked.

This was actually the 2nd time recently that I've had to go get her out of a situation she wasn't comfortable in. The previous was from a few weekends prior when her and some of her college friends went to College Station for the weekend & were supposed to head to Austin the next day for hiking. Well, the plans changed, so Morgan called me to come get her because she wasn't comfortable staying there. She was shocked when I said ok. She said, "But Mom, it's four and a half hours away." I told her it was fine since it would be good to get out of the house and take a small road trip!

The next day, we had to drive back down to Fair Park to get her purse out of the girl's car and we left her keys in it. Too bad if it gets taken crazy! We stopped for lunch in Dallas at a vegan restaurant Morgan had been wanting to try. It was fantastic! Later that afternoon, LaKisha and her family came over for dinner.

Tim returned from the lease and taught her girls how to shoot! They were all really good shots! We had a great time relaxing and visiting!

'I know ya had to go;
but please don't fade away'
'Don't Fade Away' – Bleu Edmondson

On the 8th, I posted:

ONE FINAL DOWN, 2 TO GO
THEN POOH IS HOME FOR SUMMER!

That day on Facebook, memories popped up from Lindsay and
Kendall's wedding three years prior. The video of Pierce dancing
the 'Skanky Leg' with Lindsay came up. It was bittersweet to see
him alive and dancing.

Blog about grieving moms:

**For 1 in 4 women, Mother's Day can really sting. Here is a
glimpse into the heart of a Bereaved Mother.**
To honor International Bereaved Mother's Day, we are launched
this short film. The film "We Carry Them In Our Hearts" is a worldwide collaboration of women helping to shine a light on what it is
like to experience and survive the unimaginable death of a baby or
child of any age (including adult children) or gestation.
If you are a Bereaved Mother, JOIN THE MOVEMENT
Marie -*Founder of International Bereaved Mother Day*

On the 9th, I just received a message from a mom in Georgia. Her 20-year old son took his own life at the beginning of February after battling depression & anxiety since he was 5 years old. He too, saved 5 lives through organ donation. His transplant nurse, gave them a copy of my book to read. She said it was very helpful, especially in regards to the letters we wrote to the recipients. She is in the process of reaching out to them now.

I was so touched that she would reach out to me, especially when she is still in the very beginnings of her loss. I was also surprised to learn a nurse in Georgia has my book. Definitely feeling blessed! #GodIsGoodAllTheTime

I BRUSHED MY HAIR TODAY

May 7 ⊠I brushed my hair today. For the first time in 4 weeks. It was matted and twisted together. It snapped and tore with every stroke. I cried while I washed and conditioned it, because I forgot how it felt to run my fingers through it. I brushed my teeth, too, for the first time in a week. My gums bled. My water ran red. I cried over that, as well. When I got out of the shower, I couldn't stop sniffing my hair and arms. I've avoided hugging people for a while, because I never smell good. I always smell like I've been on bed-rest for a week. I have no clean clothes, because I'm too tired and sad to wash them. Depression isn't beautiful. Depression is bad hygiene, dirty dishes, and a sore body from sleeping too much. Depression is having 3 friends that are only still around because they have the patience and love of a saint. Depression is crying until there's no more tears, just dry heaving and sobbing until you're gasping for your next breath. Depression is staring at the ceiling until your eyes burn because you forget to blink. Depression is making your family cry because they think you don't love them anymore when you're distant and distracted. Depression is somatic as well as emotional, an emptiness you can physically feel.

Please be easy on your friends and family that have trouble getting up the energy to clean, hang out, or take care of themselves. And please, please take them seriously if they talk to you about it. We're trying. I swear we're trying. See? I brushed my hair today. -By Katelyn Lesho

On the 10th, it was the Leopard Lacrosse Club's end of the year banquet. We surprised the Griffin's by showing up and did not tell them in advance that we are giving Cole the 'Bobby Pierce Forest Gilbert Memorial Scholarship'. It was an incredibly emotional night as I had the honor of presenting the award to Cole. We selected Cole, since he has demonstrated the living definition of perseverance. While many 'on the outside saw the happy-go-lucky Cole with a smile on his face', they didn't realize he was struggling with the loss of his best friend; yet, he persevered. We couldn't be more proud of him or feel happier than to give him Pierce's scholarship!

presenting scholarship to Cole

⊠s with the Griffin's

I was shocked at how emotional I got during the presentation! I didn't cry last year when I gave out the first scholarship; but, I guess since we were giving it to Cole, that's why it was so touching for me.

My blog from the 10th:
Memorial Scholarship:
Last night, Tim and I attended the Leopard Lacrosse Banquet. I started Leopard Lacrosse Club 10 years ago when Pierce wanted to play for his school/his community, not the neighboring district. Cole is the last original member of the team back when I formed it. He is also the longest player for the team, since he started as a fifth grader on the sixth grade team.

Tim and I chose to give him the 'Bobby Pierce Forest Gilbert Memorial Scholarship' since he represents the true definition of the word perseverance. Cole struggled with depression after Pierce's suicide because they were best friends. Thankfully, he made his way through it; and, will be attending the University of Dallas in the fall, where he will play lacrosse for their team.

Last year, I awarded the scholarship to Weston Haas, who was one of the original players and he now plays for BYU. When I presented the award last year, I got a little choked up, but made it through the presentation fairly well. Last night, not so much. I first got emotional when we watched the team highlight video and I saw a player wearing #22 (Pierce's number).

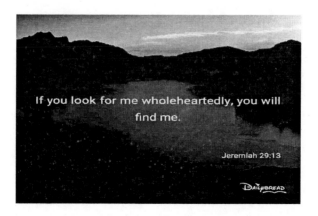

If you look for me wholeheartedly, you will find me.

Jeremiah 29:13

DailyBread

All I could think of is that should be Pierce, but, it's not.

Then, when I got on stage to present our scholarship, it went okay at first; but the second I said the words, the 'Bobby Pierce Forest Gilbert Memorial Scholarship', I lost it. I think it was so emotional because I was giving it to Pierce's best friend, who we know struggled so after his passing.

Hopefully, the one's in attendance were able to understand the rest of the speech through my tears. It was wonderful seeing him so happy last night, with his big smile and goofy actions. We're very proud of him and know he has a bright future ahead of him!

On the 12th, we left for our annual trip to St. George Island, so here's my post:

P-Diddy flying high with us to SGI!!!

I took the book, originally intending giving it to Rebecca Turk, our favorite singer from Tallahassee; but, ended up giving it to a young service member on on our flight.

'Mama always said life was like a box of chocolates - ya never know what you're gonna get' - Forest Gump

On the 12th, we had two of our friends form a golf team to participate in the Young Life Golf Tournament since we were a sponsor: Our golf team proudly represented Pierce Remodeling Group today at the Young Life golf tournament! Thanks guys! Too bad y'all LOST!

Mayor Culbertson ⊠ Carlo 'The Stallion' Strippolli

My post from the 13th:
We're proud to give two scholarships in your honor this year Mr. Weaver!! We wish all principals cared on the level you did!!! We feel so blessed you were our kids principal!! #FlyHigh

On the 14th, we had to waste time before checking into our beach house rental @ 4 that afternoon, so we had lunch at Paddy's and then ran into Rebecca Turk at a different bar afterwards. She told me every time she sings "Burning House' by Cam, she thinks of me.

I never knew how strong I was, until I had to
FORGIVE
Someone who wasn't sorry &
ACCEPT
An apology I never received

TIM'S BEACH BODY TEST
FOR THE WEE⊠ :
DO I LOO⊠ BETTER THA⊠
⊠OSH WHEATO⊠⊠
YEP⊠
LET'S HIT THE BEACH⊠
⊠I love picking on bratty-rat ⊠
bio bro⊠

The next day, news of lead singer of Soundgarden, Chris Cornell, committed suicide broke. His wife issued the following statement: Vicky Cornell, the wife of Soundgarden singer Chris Cornell, issued a statement Friday morning where she remembered her late husband, who died Thursday morning at the age of 52, and speculated whether his suicide was the result of taking too much of his anxiety medication.

"Chris's death is a loss that escapes words and has created an emptiness in my heart that will never be filled. As everyone who knew him commented, Chris was a devoted father and husband. He was my best friend," Vicky wrote.

"His world revolved around his family first and, of course, his music second. He flew home for Mother's Day to spend time with our family. He flew out mid-day Wednesday, the day of the show, after spending time with the children. When we spoke before the show, we discussed plans for a vacation over Memorial Day and other things we wanted to do."

However, following Soundgarden's concert Wednesday night, Vicky noticed a change in her husband's demeanor when they talked on the phone after the show.

"When we spoke after the show, I noticed he was slurring his words; he was different. When he told me he may have taken an extra Ativan or two, I contacted security and asked that they check on him," she continued. "What happened is inexplicable and I am hopeful that further medical reports will provide additional details. I know that he loved our children and he would not hurt them by intentionally taking his own life."

An attorney for the Cornell family, Kirk Pasich, reiterated Vicky's belief that an extra dosage of Ativan, an anxiety medication often employed by recovering addicts, altered Chris Cornell's mental faculties after the Detroit show. Pasich added that the Cornell family is "disturbed at inferences that Chris knowingly and intentionally took his life."

Every time you're feelin' empty, better thank your lucky stars;
cuz if you ever felt one breaking, you'd never want a heart.
You ain't missin' nothin', cuz love is so damn hard;
take it from me darlin', you don't want a heart.
Hey there Mr. Tin Man, glad we talked this out
You can take mine if you want it, it's in pieces now.
By the way there Mr. Tin Man, if you don't mind the scars,
you give me your armor, and you can have my heart.
'Mr. Tin Man' - Miranda Lambert

"Without the results of toxicology tests, we do not know what was going on with Chris — or if any substances contributed to his demise," Pasich said. "Chris, a recovering addict, had a prescription for Ativan and may have taken more Ativan than recommended dosages.

The family believes that if Chris took his life, he did not know what he was doing, and that drugs or other substances may have affected his actions." Pasich added that side effects of Ativan include "paranoid or suicidal thoughts, slurred speech and impaired judgment"

Vicky Cornell noted her husband's slurred speech following the Detroit concert in her statement. She added, "The outpouring of love and support from his fans, friends and family means so much more to us than anyone can know. Thank you for that, and for understanding how difficult this is for us."

Hours after Cornell's death at a Detroit hotel, a medical examiner's report confirmed that the singer had died by suicide.'

This pic was taken during our spring break trip to NYC & then a train ride to DC. P wanted to flip-off Obama in the Whighthouse, but when he saw the secret service guys, he chickened out!

To remember that night, I ain't over it yet;
The only time you cross my mind, Only all day, Only all night,
Only always, Only all the time.'
'Only All The Time' – Mike Ryan

CHRIS CORNELL: WHEN SUICIDE DOESN'T MAKE SENSE

How can these people take their own lives? In order to answer this question, we need to better understand suicide as an illness.

By Julie A. Fast

Sometimes, people die from suicide and we are able to make some sense of why it happened. It's scary and upsets our world, but on a basic level we think we understand. Robin William's suicide comes to mind. He had a history of depression and his health was failing.

Oh, how we all wish he could have found more help, but I don't think it was as much surprising as it was devastating and sad for the millions who loved him when he died.

Then there are suicides that make no sense. The behavior doesn't fit with how we see the individual's personal life or fit with how they describe their life in public. The partner or other loved ones are usually shocked and usually vehemently deny that the person was acting suicidal. Society likes to look for something deeper when they hear that the person wasn't outwardly suicidal. A possible secret life or maybe the person was lying to everyone.

I have a different opinion based on very personal experience that I would like to share.

There are many kinds of suicides. Some are societal or culturally based and accepted such as seppuku, part of the Japanese samurai bushido code of honor. For some, suicide is an act of loneliness and despair that fits with what is actually happening in life. This is suicide in reaction to life events. Then there is suicide from an ill brain. I call this brain chemical suicide. These are the people who 'have it all.' Who are getting their jobs done and sharing their lives with the public. People like Chris Cornell.

How can people who seem to have it all possibly take their lives?

In order to answer this question, we need to better understand suicide as a symptom of an illness as well as a symptom that can be quickly triggered. Instead of thinking of suicide as a conscious choice that happens when

'And lately I've been thinkin', about a boy I used to know;
he was taken from this world, at ⊠1⊠ years old
When I look up at that photograph, see that smile there on his face,
man it sure is hard to grasp; but ,I know he's in a better place.
'Cuz God's got a spot in Heaven, for good ole boys like us.
He knows wings just aren't our things, so up there they drive pickup trucks.
And as we speak, they're probably spinnin' tires and sliggin' mud; yeah
Gods got a place, yeah Gods got a place,
for good ole boys like us,'
'Good Ole Boys Like Us' - ⊠Lawhorn

someone doesn't want to live anymore, we need to see the other side of suicide. The kind of suicidal life I experience. You can easily read about me online. I'm one of the top bipolar disorder writers in the world with over 450,000 books sold. I teach bipolar disorder management. I'm incredibly open about my daily struggles with this illness. By any standard, I've got my bipolar act together. My relationships are stable. I teach the people around me to help me. I get on with life despite many physical health obstacles. I help others who are suicidal. I know what affect my suicide would have on my family and readers. You would think this would keep me immune from suicidal episodes. It doesn't.

Last year I moved to the South of France to reach a dream. I did it! I started school and began balancing my work and school life. It was going well. One day, I was sitting in my room in Cannes. I could literally hear the waves of the Mediterranean Sea outside my window. I saw gorgeous orange and yellow buildings with clay tiles. I heard the amazing sound of trains traveling from Paris going by my window. It was heaven. I had been a bit depressed for a few days, but just assumed it was from the big change I had in life. Overall, I knew I had made the right decision.

And then, I heard an overly persuasive voice say, "Julie, jump out of your window. Jump out now." In the same moment, I had an intense feeling and belief that all would be better in my life if I just killed myself. It felt as real and normal as having an inclination to go to the beach. There was nothing and I do mean nothing personal in my life to justify this kind of feeling. If you looked at my life, it made NO sense that I was suicidal. But there is something in my brain that makes sense of the situation. My mood disorder comes with suicidal depression. It gets triggered. I don't have to be down or upset. It just happens when it gets triggered. It feels as real as breathing. I hear the voice, have the thought and in my case see a movie of myself jumping all at once. Something in me simply yells, "Do it Julie! Do it!"

It's visceral. It's magnetic and hypnotic and REAL. Brain chemicals are far more powerful than any drug and when mine go off, I get suicidal. I've come close to dying many times. A few minutes later, the suicide plan I created for myself 20 years ago allowed me to see through this chemical episode and I got immediate help. Not everyone has a plan to counteract chemical suicidal thoughts, but I do.

When you don't have a plan that helps these sudden and inexplicable suicidal thoughts, the resulting suicide can never be explained by what is going on in life.

My post from the 20th:
On the 20th, it was the 2nd Chance Run in the Stockyards. We had originally planned on cutting our trip short to attend the event; but, decided at the last minute to stay the full 10 days.

Team Pierce has a good turnout.

Three of his recipients were in attendance:
Alicia (left kidney/pancreas)
David Ray (heart)
Christina (liver)
Bryant (lungs) was unable to make it since he lives in Odessa.

We decided that is what we needed for us at that time. I, of course, felt guilty for not going back; but as Tim pointed out to me, if all you ever do is give of yourself and don't take time for yourself, you'll have nothing left to give.
On the 20th, it was our last day at the beach, so I went on one last walk on the beach. I took this pic at the break point @ SGI proudly representing P-Diddy in his Luckenbach hat (or as he called it as a kid Lucky-back!)-

Representing P wi his Luckenbauch hat!
Thanks SGI! Ya treated us right...12 years & counting!

On the 21st, before leaving the island, we stopped and had brunch. Rebecca was performing and I cried when she sang 'Tin Man' by Miranda Lambert; and of course, she sang 'Burning House' by Cam for me too!

Upon returning home, I was contacted by Jeanna, who runs the non-profit NEWCO of Grayson County. She asked me to be a guest speaker at the mental health conference in February. They hosted a conference in September; but, Austin College only had capacity for 300 people, so they had to turn away people. So, in February, it will be held at the Hilton in Sherman. At the conference in September, she had five different people approach her, asking her if she's heard of 'the book'? When she got home that night, she looked into it and started following me. On Mother's Day, she finally read my book and couldn't put it down; and, she agrees 100⬛ with everything I wrote in it. She really wants me to be a guest speaker, as to put a 'local face' on depression and suicide. She asked me to pray about it and consider it.

At first, she was hesitant to approach me since it's only been two years and she didn't know if I'd be ready to do something like this yet; but, when running errands with her kids, she found two dimes and two pennies. So, she picked them up and said, "Okay Pierce, I'll call her." Her kids asked her who she was talking to and she replied, "You wouldn't believe me if I told you!"

Needless to say, I accepted the invitation and am beyond honored and thrilled to be a participant at such a great event! The NEWCO group was found by Mrs. Huffins', who is a champion for mental health and awareness! Numerous law enforcement officers, doctors, nurses and teacher participate in these programs. After the speeches, we will break off into groups and do a question & answer section.

Mid-month, Tim took his truck into the Ford dealership in Sherman to have the oil changed. A young lady who works there, approached him as he was leaving saying, "I thought I recognized you, you're Bobbi's husband." Tim said, "Yeah, I thought I recognized you too." She went on to explain that she's the one that I talk to on FB all the time. She messaged me after Tim left; and said while speaking to him, she almost burst into tears while talking to Tim because he and P are so much alike, it was like talking to P again!

What's funny is that she looks like Karli, P's first love! Too bad they couldn't have worked out. She's the girl P started talking to during one of the many brake-ups with Sarah. They had plans to start dating once she turned 18; but then, P suddenly broke off all communications with her. Unknowingly to her, it was because Sarah found out about her and came running back to P. When she found out why, she told him he was pathetic for getting back together with her!

On the 25th, a new campaign aired here in N. Texas promoting mental health awareness. The jest of the ad is 'it's okay for me to say I have heart disease, why not depression.' Okaytosay.org is the group and Emmitt Smith, former running back for the Dallas Cowboys and Mark Cuban, owner of the Dallas Mavericks, participated in the the commercial! So excited to see this promo! ⊠*okaytosay*

To My Baby Girl, No Matter Where Life Takes You, Mommy Has Your Back

Did you know that I used to talk to you before you were born? I used to sing to you and tell you how much I loved you!

I never loved anyone as much as I love you! I was young and scared. And whether I was ready or not you were coming. I wondered if I would be a good mom or not. I still question that every day. But I try to do my best for you! I try to work hard and better myself for you!

Do you know how special you are? You brighten everybody's day! You are so beautiful, so sweet. My little angel. You have blessed my life so much.

I believe you have kept me safe from harm. You have given me hope for better days. You are truly a blessing I hope you know that.

Mommy loves you.

No matter where life takes you I have your back. Whatever choices you make good or bad I may not always agree with them but I will be here through it all. I will not judge you for your mistakes. We all make them, and god knows I have made my own set of mistakes.

You can count on me. I know that even though you are only two years old you've been through A lot of changes already. I promise I will explain it all to you one day.

I hope you never resent me for trying to take care of you the best way that I know how. I pray that life is kind to you. And that even though I know you will have challenges I hope that they will never be as hard as mine were.

You deserve the very best and I will fight for you. I will protect you. I will love you without conditions because you are the love of my life. Whatever you do be strong, and never give up. If you find yourself feeling alone or sad you can turn to me. I will wipe your tears and hold you close.

Mommy loves you so much.

I hope you have ambition! I hope you make it far in life and that all your dreams come true. No matter what I hope you can learn to love yourself.

People are mean and the world is cold, but don't let them dim the light in your sparkly brown eyes.

You're so special to me. I just want you to know that. You are my whole world.

Mommy loves you forever and always.

– by Nicole on PuckerMom

On May 27th, Gov. Greg Abbott of Texas signed a bill cracking down on teacher/student relationships, stating:

'This type of behavior is unacceptable, and Texas will protect its children from sexual predators in our classrooms. Texas schools should be safe places for our children to learn and advance.'

Your day is coming, your time is near, your dreams are closer than you know. Keep hope. One day at a time, my friend.

Brendon Burchard

Luv this pic of Pierce since it shows off his freckles! My mom's best friend, Evelyn, told him when he was little, that they were left there from when angels kissed him!

From my blog on my site
www.SurvivingOurSonsSuicide.com
Depression is the #1 leading cause of death in the WORLD:
When Margaret Chan, leader of the World Health Organization, declared that depression is the #1 leading cause of death in the world, not cancer, that should tell you it is an epidemic.
When someone dies from depression, it is suicide. Suicide is the 4th leading cause of death for 10 - 14 year olds and the 2nd leading cause of death for 15- 24 year olds.
I find it odd, that our public schools in Texas, will allow MADD to stage a horrific reenactment of a deadly car crash the week before

prom, but SHHHH....don't talk about suicide! When our 8th graders receive the sex education awareness and the suicide awareness program in the same week, and their take on it is that the sex talk was much easier, why is this? It's due to the fact that sex has been de-stigmatize because it is so often spoken about, seen in movies, TV programs, publications, etc.

So what if, we as parents and educators, talk so much about suicide, depression and mental health, we de-stigmatize it?

How is a child/student going to know it's okay to say I'm not ok, if we don't discuss it with them. They don't know how to say how they are feeling or what's going on with them inside and they often feel as if they are the only one experiencing this; thus, leading to self medicating and self harm.

I propose we have the suicide awareness program in September, during suicide awareness month. Have our school counselors give a pre-screening test to help identify which students are struggling. Also, before each holiday break, send home a flyer with the warning signs, along with the suicide hot-line number on it. The majority of suicides occur during or right after a holiday break. As parents and educators, we need to teach our children coping skills. Not every one is going to make the team, get the lead in the play, be first seat in band. Not every kids is going to be top 10⊠ . Not every kid is going to get into their first choice for college. Every kid will, as we all know, experience heart break, failure, rejection, stress, pressure to succeed, per pressure, and loneliness. We have to teach them coping skills or they won't know how to cope; to realize, there's always tomorrow.

As I tell students at my speeches, if you only take one thing away from this, know that **SUICIDE IS A PERMANENT SOLUTION TO A TEMPORARY PROBLEM.**

We had planned on attending P's best friend's graduation party on the 27th, but I just can't handle it. I can't bear driving through our old town, seeing all the congrats to our grad parties, etc. So, I decided to deliver grad gifts the following week when I'm in town. #onestepforwardtwostepsback

Over Memorial Day weekend, Morgan went to Austin to spend the weekend with her cousin Caitlin. We were so excited for her to get to go down to the hill country and hike, relax, and visit!

On Saturday, Morgan called me screaming and crying saying, "I got in! I got in Mom! Texas State just e-mailed saying I've been accepted for the fall!" She was literally crying tears of joy! We're so excited for her new adventures!!!

P's Memorial Day Gift to me!

My blog from the 29th:
Graduation Part2:
Well, we had good intentions of attending Pierce's best friend's graduation party yesterday; but when the moment came around to time to get ready, I just couldn't. The old familiar feeling - of the rod between my shoulder blades - came back. I've come to recognize this as a 'sign' of impending doom...something is not right, it's something I shouldn't do.
So at the last minute, I made the decision not to go. I realized that being in a party type atmosphere would not be good for me. Yes, I want to celebrate with Cole, but not all the others.
I don't want to pretend that everything is great, perfect, okay; because for us, it's not. That's the bottom line, simple, very raw, truth of the matter. We will, celebrate with Cole and his parents, in a private setting this next week; which will be great.
When things hit you unexpectedly, out of the blue, it's hard to

know how to react...do you 'buck up' and do what's expected...but now, two years into our journey of surviving Pierce's suicide, I've come to the realization that I have to start making choices that are right for me, my mental health, or there won't be anything left of me to give.

#TeamPierce
#heldtogetherwithducttapetissuesandprayers

'Boy, your gonna know it all, you'll think you're ten feet tall,
and run like your bulletproof, and total a car or two.
You're gonna drive and kiss, and throw a punch and
grow up way too fast. You're gonna drop the ball,
hit a wall ,and break some hearts like glass.
I know you will, 'cause you're a part of me,
and part of you will always be a ....boy.

....but boy, your gonna love 1⊠, and boy you'll do some stupid things.

Boy, you're gonna be so stubborn, you get that from your mother, I already see
it now, you weren't built for backing down.'
'Boy' - Lee Brice

Blog post:
Sadness:
In my previous blog, I mentioned that this past weekend, with it being graduation for several of Pierce's friends, that it hit me hard and I was upset for several days. Yesterday, Morgan and I ran errands and dropped off several grad gifts while in town. Before we left, she asked me what was wrong. I told her I was just bummed, but I'd be okay. Later that afternoon, she said to me, "I need you to be okay, not in a funk. I need you to be happy."
I think it concerned her because when she's been home I'm 'happy' the majority of the time. She doesn't see me when the sadness creeps back in, so I think it scared her. But, not being a parent, she doesn't comprehend that this is something that is never truly going to go away. That my heart will never completely mend.

It just dawned on me that this was the last photo ever taken of P. It was us at the Randy Rogers/Josh Abbott concert at WinStar in Oklahoma - two weeks prior to his death.

My friend LaKisha posted & tagged me in this on the 29th:
I just want to take a moment and tell you that you give me hope. You make me wanna be a better me; not just for my kids, but for myself also!!! You reassure me that I am great and to know I have someone like you in my corner brings me so much joy!!!
So I say thank you! Thank you for being your strong beautiful amazing self my friend!!!
#sheisthedefinitionofhope#sheisstrength#shisknowledge

On the 30th, I saw a post from a girl saying: 'Let's play a 13 reasons why game. Comment & I'll reply 'tape' if you've hurt me & then you'll have to figure out why'.
My reply:
That's so sick!!! Being a parent who is surviving the suicide of our 17-yr old son 2 years ago due to a toxic relationship w/ a girl who used him for 9 months - how dare you? Mental health IS NOT A GAME!!!!!!!!

The Lord is close to the broken hearted;
And saves those who are crushed in spirit. -Psalm 34:18

Forest Gump⊠ white suit at the Bubba Gump Shrimp Co. in N⊠ LA

June 2017

On the first, we met the Griffins for dinner in downtown McKinney to celebrate Cole's graduation. Olivia is overseas for an internship with the UN, so it was just the 6 of us. We had a great evening and we also celebrated Morgan's acceptance into Texas State!

kissing our graduate

On the 3rd, I temporarily took my book off line so that I could make corrections to it from the first run, add reviews in the beginning and a forward written for me by Jeanna of NEWCO of Grayson County.

On the 4th, we went to Big D and stayed in the Adolphus Hotel to celebrate our 23rd anniversary! It was a great night. Then the next morning, while having brunch, we chatted with the couple at the next table. It turns out, I graduated high school with the guy! Small world!!

I got a message from our favorite singer/songwriter, Rebecca Turk: I got your book! I'm visiting home right now and thought I'd send a pic of my mom reading it. I played her the song too. Your book is very powerful. It's amazing that you have been able to share your tragedy and experience with others! We prayed for you and your family!

On a Saturday night, there wasn't any of our shows recorded, so we flipped through the stations and ended up viewing two of Pierce's favorite movies. The first one was 'American Sniper' with Bradley Cooper. I was immediately filled with the recollection of seeing it at the theater with Pierce. I recall how incredibly, deeply, it touched/bothered him; as his mom, even without words being spoken between us, leaving the theater that night, I saw the incredible sadness in him. His intelligent mind, not being able to wrap his brain around how someone, out of the goodness/kindness of their heart, could be killed while trying to help others. It literally shook him to his core. Then, you have the flip side of him, the humor; which he got from me, (yes, Tim has it as well - but there was a special sense of humor he & I shared) Talladega Nights played (which was a needed relief after the first movie). It's odd to me to watch previously seen shows, view them, and recall things. I know he was laughing with us.

On the 6th, I went with Morgan to Stephenville to clear out her apartment; since' she won't be returning there for the fall. On the way home, we stopped in Ft. Worth and had dinner with Mama. Morgan loved seeing her MeeMaw and said how much she loves and misses her!

While we were gone, there was a horrible accident on Hwy 121 here in the Texoma area. Tim came upon it shortly after it happened; he realized, there had to be fatalities with how badly some of the cars were damaged. He said a prayer for the ones who lost their lives, for their families, and friends. We found out later that two teen-age girls from Anna did not survive. Also, two grandparents who were returning from their granddaughter's dance recital, passed.

The granddaughter was taken by Care Flight, along with her mom, who was 8 months pregnant; they delivered the baby early to save it; but, sadly, the mom didn't survive. P played Three Doors Down's 'When I'm Gone' for me tonight, knowing how upset we were learning about the 2 local teens killed in the tragic accident. He told Tim he was the 'newest' one from our area up there; so, he gets to show them the ropes upon arrival.

My blog on the 7th:
Moving back home for summer:
Today, I went with Morgan to Stephenville to load up what was left of her apartment, since she has has been accepted to Texas State for the fall. We had a great day together. I finally got to meet her best friend, Tyler; and seeing them together, laughing and picking on each other, so reminds me of me and Steven (my best friend since 6th grade) and I can see it will be a life-long friendship.
We arrived at the apartment and spent 2 hours packing up her belongings and then loading them into the truck. On our way back home, we met Mama in Ft. Worth for dinner. Morgan was SO excited to have dinner with her, stating how much she has missed her MeeMaw.
I'm so thankful for these 'milestone' moments: seeing her move on to her next steps, seeing pure joy and happiness in her again for she so deeply deserves it!

Pierce's piercing eyes made his name even more perfect
than just being a 5th generation family name!

'I woke up before the sun, chased your ghost across the yard.
Through the fog and tumbling dark, 'til you were gone.
Virginia, I can hardly breath, and I've forgotten how to sleep,
and your face still haunts my dreams when I'm alone.
So now I'm walking on a tightrope wire,
too far off the ground.
I'm imagining the words you said,
when last I saw your mouth.
'Tightrope' Ron Pope

My blog:

Viewing sadness in society:

With my advocacy, needing to promote my mission of suicide awareness, I have used my original Facebook Page to promote my book, my site, etc; thus, I now have over 5k followers.

In this endeavor, I have seen, what I consider to be, an alarming rate of people posting truly sad, desperate, lost, hopeless, etc type remarks. This, for me, being in the situation we are in, dealing with our son's suicide 2 years ago, breaks my heart into more tiny pieces. For all who are struggling, there is hope. THERE IS HELP!

As I say in my speeches to youth and PTA's: SUICIDE IS A PERMANENT SOLUTION TO A TEMPORARY PROBLEM. Although it is not the intent of the one taking their own life to relieve their pain, they unknowingly release it to their friends and loved ones. Ask for help please!

THERE IS ALWAYS TOMORROW!

SUICIDE HOTLINE
1-800-273-8255

Tim and I are praying together for the parents of Anna, Texas, that lost their teenage daughters in a horrific crash this afternoon on Hwy 121. We sadly know, the depths of their loss and pray for peace, comfort, love, and support for all of them, including their family members, friends, first responders, and the community as a whole. May God bless each of you in the following days, weeks, months, years, etc. Hold tight to God's love, knowing they are in Heaven and at peace.

TEXOMA YOUTH WHO LOST FRIENDS TODAY
CLING TO ONE ANOTHER
HANG IN THERE
DON'T GIVE UP HOPE!
CRISIS HOTLINE:
800-273-8255

I ordered personalized plates for my & Tim's vehicles. Both are a combination of P's initials w/ his number 22. Today, Tim gave an estimate to a potential client. When he got home, he received a text from the home owner, asking, "I noticed your personal plates & can't seem to figure it out. What does it stand for?"

Of course our typical reaction to those who don't know is, delay.... Then the reply, 'it's a tribute to our son - his initials & the numbers from his jersey.'
No reply as of yet.......Shock & Awe!

From The Samaritan Inn's site:

Dear Friend,

School is out and summer is in full swing!

Often times, school is the only gleam of socialization that at-risk children receive. There, they can engage with friends at lunch, use recess as an outlet to be active, and count on lesson plans to stimulate their minds. When those school doors close, many of them are faced with the television being their only source of entertainment, and when you're living in a homeless shelter, even that luxury isn't always an option.

Years ago, the Samaritan Inn began the Sponsor a Child campaign so that we could provide the kids of the Inn a fun and educational summer outside of the shelter. With your help, we created the ultimate gift: the feeling of endless possibilities and memories that will last a lifetime. Many of these children will experience exciting "firsts" like swimming, horseback riding, and going to a theme park. To some, the experiences will be life-changing.

Take a look at this letter from one of last year's teen campers. Kendall also participated in an essay contest, sharing her meaningful camp experiences, and won a laptop for college. Child sponsorship is the most personal way to fight against homelessness. When you sponsor a child, you are giving a homeless child the summer you want for your own children. Please help us keep this program going by clicking here.

We have participated in the program for several years now, starting about that time our kids stopped participating in summer programs. I feel it's so important to get the kids out of the shelter and let them experience things they may not otherwise get to, like horseback riding!

'To remember that night,
I ain't over it yet;
The only time you cross my mind,
Only all day, Only all night
Only always.'
'Only All The Time' - Mike Ryan

This was P's last time @ the lease. On the way down, he was driving & he didn't realize Tim turned on the heated seat. After a few hours, he commented that his butt was sweating and couldn't figure out why! He shot two bucks that weekend.

June 7

I AM ALL AROUND YOU, like a cocoon of Light. My Presence with you is a promise, independent of your awareness of Me. Many things can block this awareness, but the major culprit is worry. My children tend to accept worry as an inescapable fact of life. However, worry is a form of unbelief; it is anathema to Me.

Who is in charge of your life? If it is you, then you have good reason to worry. But since I am in charge, worry is both unnecessary and counterproductive. When you start to feel anxious about something, relinquish the situation to Me. Back off a bit, redirecting your focus to Me. I will either take care of the problem Myself or show you how to handle it. In this world you will have problems, but you need not lose sight of Me.

LUKE 12:22–31; JOHN 16:33

Just a little FYI:
Did you know that if you text HOME to 741741 when you are depressed, suicidal, or just needing someone to talk to, a real Crisis Counselor will text you until you are good? Everyone doesn't like talking on the phone. Spread the word. It's a free service. This may save someone's life who isn't comfortable calling.

Organ Recipient Accepts Diploma on Behalf of 13-Year-Old Who Donated Liver

GALT -- Parents, grandparents -- so many proud and smiling faces at the McCaffrey Middle School eighth-grade promotion ceremony. But one family is in tears.

Eric Blackwell, 35, walks up on stage to accept the last diploma. But it's not for him. It's for the boy who saved his life.

"How amazing this opportunity was. And how rare it was," Blackwell said. On March 11, 13-year-old Michael Balsley-Rodriguez died after accidentally shooting himself. He never got to live out his dreams of becoming a football coach. After the tragedy, Michael's parents vowed to have their son live on through the gift of life.

"The actual liver is right here," Blackwell said.

Last May, Blackwell was diagnosed with stage 3 liver cancer. Doctors gave him three years to live. The odds were not in his favor.

"I was number 5,000 something on the list, so it may have been six years," Blackwell said.

Then on March 11, he got a call. Michael was a near perfect match. And as fate would have it, Blackwell is a football coach for the same team Michael played on. Just in a different age division. "Everything coming together, it's like wow. It's almost like it was meant to be in some kind of way," said Michael's mother, Silvia Vansteyn.

For Michael's mother, hearing her son's name at graduation was bittersweet. But knowing he saved Blackwell's life meant the world.

"Michael is inside of him, and I actually got to hug him today. And it was pretty cool," Vansteyn said.

"Michael wanted to be a football coach. And now he can live inside of me, and continue his legacy to be that,"Blackwell said. "In this tragedy, something good came out of it," Vansteyn said.

My post from the 12th:

Challenge #Accepted!! - So here it goes! If I didn't tag you, please don't be offended. I tried to pick people who I think would play along!

All too often.. #we women, find it easier to criticize each other instead of building each other up. With all the negativity going around let's do something positive!! Upload 1 picture of yourself.. #ONLY you. Then tag 25 or more gorgeous women to do the same. Build yourself up instead of tearing yourself down.

'Damn the rain, for making me remember,
all the pain, from losing everything,
still miss her touch, still love her too much,
so damn the rain⊠
'Damn The Rain' – Randy Rogers Band

From my blog:

Life- long friends:

Tonight, it's great having Robbie here. He is Morgan's best friend from 7th grade. He's the one I often refer to as my son-from-a-different-mudder. It's so great having him here, filling the void – the void left by P's choice that night, to take his life. Sigh......

that killer smile

I just saw a new review of my book on Amazon-Review of 'Our Year of First Without You' A journey through suicide and organ donation:

5.0 out of 5 stars This book has blessed me.
By Kristi K. on June 11, 2017
Format: Kindle Edition Verified Purchase
I haven't quite finished reading this but have felt so blessed to learn your family's story, as I have dealt with mental illness & a failed attempt and have a younger cousin who took his own life. I first learned about Pierce through keeping up with a high school classmate of mine, who received TWO of his organs. Looking through her recent wedding photos I started thinking how "lucky" she was (after all, she is such a beautiful soul) to finally get her happy ever after. As I was looking through her older photos, it led to your page, Bobbi, and I just started looking and reading and when I learned Pierce had taken his life my heart broke for your family and I knew I needed to read this. I would suggest this book for anyone who has loved, lost, struggled with faith, seen God's power. It's truly a beautiful work.

taken at LaX tournament in Shreveport

This is one of the best explanations I've read on depression!
Taken from the site 'Depression Kills":

"The so-called 'psychotically depressed' person who tries to kill herself doesn't do so out of quote 'hopelessness' or any abstract conviction that life's assets and debits do not square. And surely not because death seems suddenly appealing. The person in whom Its invisible agony reaches a certain unendurable level will kill herself the same way a trapped person will eventually jump from the window of a burning high-rise. Make no mistake about people who leap from burning windows. Their terror of falling from a great height is still just as great as it would be for you or me standing speculatively at the same window just checking out the view; i.e. the fear of falling remains a constant. The variable here is the other terror, the fire's flames: when the flames get close enough, falling to death becomes the slightly less terrible of two terrors. It's not desiring the fall; it's terror of the flames. Yet nobody down on the sidewalk, looking up and yelling 'Don't!' and 'Hang on!', can understand the jump. Not really. You'd have to have personally been trapped and felt flames to really understand a terror way beyond falling." -David Foster Wallace

From my blog:
Second book:
So many have told me, since my first book, that there needs to be a second one since so much has happened since, that still pertains to our journey without Pierce.

The title is ";Living Without You" which was inspired by what Tim said to me on the one year mark. He said, "We survived losing him; now, we have to survive living without him."

Which, is very true. The pain of losing him was horrific; but the pain/realization of having to live the rest of our lives without him is even more devastating. Waking up, each day, knowing you aren't going to get to see his smile, hear his laugh, hear his boots

stomping across the floor.... Wondering what he'd be doing now.

Would he have just completed his first year at McPherson College in their auto restoration program? Would he have stayed behind, worked for our company and interned with different auto people we know?

It's the what will never be that gets to you.

On the 11th, I started a 30 Day Thankful Challenge:

Starting the 30 Day Thankful Challenge:

Day 1) Morgan Kay –
She continually amazes me with her tenacity, resiliency, bravery, out-look, hopes, dreams, dedication, motivation, etc! I AM SO INCREDIBLY PROUD OF HER; the person she has fought to become, the no-looking-back-in-the-review chick, the choices she has made, her GPA (like I EVER had that in college), and her feisty, take no shit attitude!!!!!! You rock it Pooh-ella!!!!!

Day 2 of the 30 Day Thankful Challenge:
Pierce, Guido, Bubba-luv, P-Diddy, Sugar, Babe
I am so thankful I got to be your mom for 17 years and 27 days.
You brought happiness, love, laughter, exploring, questioning,
logic, stubbornness, humor, challenges, reasoning, tenacity, jokes,
boy-stuff, hugs, killer smile, and that famous laugh into our lives -
not to mention being Bee-gun's life-long best friend! Thank you for
watching over us from Heaven.

On the 12th, Jeanna e-mailed me the forward for my book. (She said, 'of course I had to re-read it first; then, felt compelled to give it to a youth who is struggling, no doubt Pierce led me to do that.)'

As a parent, I can't fathom. As a community advocate for mental health, I was humbled by the emotionally raw account of Pierce's situation. Every day the statistics grow with individuals who have mental health issues. The rise in homeless individuals battling this disease, a veteran struggling to reconnect, a mom fighting depression, and youth fighting a myriad group of life circumstances that result in making an irrevocable decision. This disease picks not specific gender, demographics, or socioeconomic status. It is unprejudiced. Pierce's mom opens herself and her family's life for us to see the bravery, the tears, the strength, and the unity that came out of this situation. Her strength and determination to educate, to advocate, and to open the doors for this taboo discussion is incredible.

A must read for anyone that deals with middle school aged to high school students, parents, clergy, and anyone engaged in the mental health field. You will gain strength, insight, and hopefully, intuition to go with your gut instinct and take action.

-Jeanna Peters- NEWCO of Grayson County

taken our first trip in N'Awlins

Impact:

So many people considered Pierce to be their best friend. He had so many friends, many we were unaware of because he only brought around the one's he thought we could help. He had long lasting friendships. He had a wide variety of friends. We were shocked at the turn out at his service and visitation.

Even after his suicide, I've had people contact me, letting me know they were friends and how much they miss him.

I found a note at his grave, written by a former classmate from MCA. In it, she expressed the impact he made in her life; by teaching her there wasn't a sin God would not forgive her for; that suicide was the cowards way out (if he had only taken his own advice); and that even though she claimed she wasn't a Christian anymore, he told her that God still loves her.#ProudToBeHisMom#TeamPierce

Day 3 of Thankful Challenge:
Timbo

We've been together now longer than we've been apart. We've been married 23 years and dated 6 before that. He is my best friend, father of our 2 kids, great Christian, who lives his life with ethics and integrity, and runs his business' the same way. He is a great dad, who often lends his insight to me in parenting when I'm 'to close to see' the issue at hand. He was Pierce's hero and role model. He's Morgan's prince charming. I can't imagine surviving the last two years without him. Thank you God for blessing me with him!

THE DAY AFTER I KILLED MYSELF

by Victoria Kroll

Last night was too much. I couldn't bare another night of crying myself to sleep, of screaming into my pillow and praying for the pain to stop. I was tired. Tired of being sad. Tired of not being able to get out of bed. Tired of nobody caring. I was tired of being alone, but also hated being with others, because they couldn't understand the constant pain I was in. So I killed myself.

The next morning, the sun rose, the birds sang, and the frost melted. My loved ones woke up, and with a good night's sleep my best friend forgot about the stupid argument we'd had the night before, the kids that teased me in the hallway had other things to worry about, and my mom, after having time to think about it, decided to hear my side of things before making the decision that I felt was so unfair. The boy that broke my heart was just another face in the crowd, because I'd had time to heal. My therapist had a great session planned for us to make another breakthrough with my depression, and my psychiatrist had a new medicine in mind for me to try.

A new kid moved in down the street who was also in need of friends, and we had so much in common. She could be my best friend. But I would never know, because I killed myself last night. My loved ones worlds' were ripped apart–my mother felt like her entire Earth was shattered, my brother decided once and for all that the world was against him, and my Grandparents (who have always had a deep faith) felt that God had forsaken them.

My friends went through every interaction we'd had for the last week, analyzing it, thinking how they should've known, how they could've stopped me, how if only they would've done something. They will never be the same.

My teammates were shocked and confused. They thought our bond was deep, how could I have been struggling and not let a single one of them know it?

The teachers at my school and the mentors/coaches in my community were in a state of shock. How could this have happened? How could a child they spent their entire day investing in have gone to such a place without them knowing? Some thought back to my vacant expression over the last few days and thought "I could've been there for her."

All the people who I had thought forgot I existed banded together. There was a candlelit vigil at my school and a celebration of life on my campus.

So many people came out and shared stories of how I had touched their lives. I will never know the positive impact I had on others, because I took that chance away from myself.

My community rallied around my memory and vowed not to let another child go down the same path. They posted Facebook statuses with suicide hotline numbers and promised to talk to their kids about their feelings. I could've talked to my loved ones about my feelings, but that felt too impossible, so instead, I killed myself.

But I wasn't there – not for the vigils, the remembrance of life, the funeral. I wasn't there for the day my brother got married. I will never graduate college and change lives like I'd always dreamed. I'm not going to be a wife and mother to the most incredible family I could ever imagine. My life ended before these people were able to show me how much they loved me. I never got to experience life on the right medications with consistent therapy. I never saw the sun come up and the storm clouds drift away.

And I Never Will

Because I killed myself.

"Suicide does not end the pain you're in, it only guarantees that it will never get better."

Some thought back to my vacant expression over the last few days and thought "I could've been there for her."

All the people who I had thought forgot I existed banded together. There was a candlelit vigil at my school and a celebration of life on my campus. So many people came out and shared stories of how I had touched their lives. I will never know the positive impact I had on others, because I took that chance away from myself.

My community rallied around my memory and vowed not to let another child go down the same path. They posted Facebook statuses with suicide hotline numbers and promised to talk to their kids about their feelings. I could've talked to my loved ones about my feelings; but, that felt too impossible, so instead, I killed myself.

But I wasn't there

– not for the vigils, the remembrance of life, the funeral.

I wasn't there for the day my brother got married.

I will never graduate college and change lives like I'd always dreamed.

I'm not going to be a wife and mother to the most incredible family I could ever imagine.

My life ended before these people were able to show me how much they loved me. I never got to experience life on the right medications with consistent therapy. I never saw the sun come up and the storm clouds drift away.

And I Never Will

Because I killed myself.

"Suicide does not end the pain you're in, it only guarantees that it will never get better."

Those words resonated with me when I was at my worst because they are so true. Sometimes suicide feels like the only way out, but it's not. The only true way to beat the pain is to go to therapy; to take your meds, and to never give up. Because one day, I promise you, it will all be worth it. From one survivor to another, **YOU CAN DO THIS!**

'Rest me in the sunshine,
soak me in the rain;
the smell of hate surrounds me,
and I want to love again.
Wrap me in the feathers lost from angel's wings,
oh they've broken my reflection,
yes, they've broken my reflection,
they've broken my reflection,
and I am in need.'
'Broken Reflection' - Wade Bowen

Is it really atrip to NYC if ya don't get a pic with the toy soldier?

Day 4 of Thankfulness Challenge:
Sonia and Joe:

They have become some of very best friends! We met Sonia when we dined at her restaurant in old downtown McKinney, the night we celebrated buying our ranch. She has a magnetic personality that draws you in; thus, we quickly built a friendship. After Pierce died and I couldn't find my phone, she had texted me several times and never got a response; so, she told Joe that if she didn't hear from me, she was going to come out the ranch to see what was wrong. When I got my replacement phone, she texted & I replied. She invited me to lunch, but that was when I still didn't want to leave the ranch, so I invited her out here. When she arrived, she could tell something was wrong & I broke the news to her. They have both clung to us - not run from us. We spend weekend nights together, sharing food and laughter. We are truly blessed to count them as friends!

'What are you out doing, what are you out for;
don't see much of you, around here anymore⊠
I guess it's just as well.

Once upon a time, you had it all.
You let everybody down⊠ You're always 1⊠
Yeah you're always 1⊠,
You're always 1⊠, in your hometown.

Running from your folks, running from the law.
Running from regrets, running from it all.
You keep on running boy, you run yourself in the ground.

Yeah your always 1⊠, your always 1⊠,
you're always 1⊠ in your hometown'
– 1⊠ Cross Canadian Ragweed

Day 5 of Thankfulness Challenge:
Jenn and Britt

Jenn LITERALLY TOOK OVER IN ALL REGARDS pertaining to Morgan after Pierce's suicide. We were so paralyzed by everything; thus, what a tremendous blessing to have her step in with the school district and arrange everything for her return and insuring she'd still be able to graduate!

Britt - he 2nd co-chairs acting as her dad.

He continually calls her to the mat over stupid decisions; holds her accountable; and would literally KILL for her!

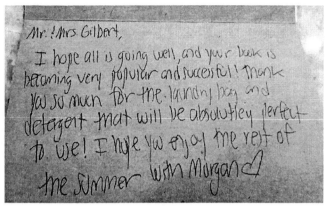

received this thank you card today!

Day 6 of Thankfulness Challenge:
This chick right here!

Where to begin is hard to figure, so I'll start with us meeting at lacrosse practice when Little David and P played together! She'd sit in her car with John and I was always there helping out, so we got to the point we'd chat while we waited for it to be over.

She has been such a HUGE inspiration in my life! She has one of the most beautiful souls I have ever been blessed with knowing! She cares oh so deeply - not just for her family, but for her friends, the community, for the underprivileged, for so many.

Not only is she wicked smart, she has one of the best senses of humor and don't even get started in a texting cut down war cuz GEEZ - she's lightening fast!!!!!!

She has been a great influence on Morgan and gives her FABULOUS guidance
and advice.

She rushed to me after P and has never left! Thankful is an understatement when it comes to counting her as one of my best friends!

Look! Cheryl had a fur baby!

Tomorrow is my daddy's birthday. Buy him beef jerky please!

On the 16th, Sonia and Joe came over to help us celebrate Tim's birthday! Morgan cooked dinner for us; she prepared, Vegan Shepard's Pie, and it was fabulous! Sonia made Tim's favorite cake.

Sonia lighting the candles on Tim's cake

That evening, I got the biggest compliment of my life it was when Joe said, " you gave Farrah a graduation gift; yet, you only met her once, I don't understand it." Tim's reply was, 'her love of giving far exceeds her bounds of personal friendships'. For me, just like Pierce, we would rather give than receive!! P and I get/got SO MUCH MORE JOY OUT OF GIVING vs receiving; thus, that is my hope that this is a part of his legacy!!!!!!!

Hot LaX Game

From my blog:

Possessions:

As I sit here, on a cool June late night evening, in Texas, which comes as a surprise considering how miserable the hot humid day was, I find myself reflecting; reflecting on different people asking me, 'you've given so much of Pierce's possessions away, what would you never give away?'

For me, that is simple:

I'D NEVER GIVE AWAY HIS:

Cross Necklace (that Tim now wears.);

his class ring (that Morgan has);

his belt with belt-buckle (that I have);

his duck commander PJ bottoms that I have and wear; his last Leopard Lacrosse jersey; his cologne; & several shirts.

Yes, we gave certain items of his to certain people - shorts/jeans/clothes to his buddies; his TV to a friend; his bedroom furniture to another friend; his truck to our foreman who is like family to us; his Mustang to his heart recipient, his original lacrosse jersey to his cousin in Chicago; his Bucky Beaver to his other cousin in Chicago.

But, I promise, with as much as I share, of our lives, you have no clue what I keep - what is held just for us. What is private.

I feel compelled to share our life with everyone in hopes of preventing another person from taking their own life; in hopes of letting survivors know they can survive. Yet, there will always be a HUGE part of our life that is just for us.

My post that night:

As I sit here in the middle of the night, not wanting to go to sleep, because sitting on the porch, with a cool breeze blowing, after the hot, humid day, I sit in the peace and quiet of the evening/morning. It's just me, being, just me and my thoughts, not caught up in life.....

I silently say a prayer, thanking God for our life and for blessing me with our life, surrounded by his creation, thankful for the beauty he surrounds us with living in the country.

I know to many, it may seem odd, that I can be thankful; considering, our past two years of surviving Pierce's suicide.

Yet, I am.

I am thankful.

Tonight, we celebrated Tim's 48th birthday with great friends and Morgan cooked dinner for us. Tonight, there was pure joy and happiness in our home - despite what we've survived.

Tonight we lived, loved, and laughed.

Thus, I am grateful, thankful, and hopeful!

Day 7 of Thankfulness Challenge:

Oh no!!!!! Wait for it!!: THE GRIFFIN'S!!!

(imagine this statement being made in P's sarcastic voice)

Well, obviously Corn-ho-li-o would be first up to bat since he was P's partner-in-crime (often referred to as Bee-vus and Butt-head) or as we affectionately called them 'the village idiots'. You two were untouchable in the bizarre humor category! You two together were almost too much for color TV!!!

Daddy David - P so loved trying to tell you how to drive the 'cedes!!! His fav memory of you was skate boardin' in Cali!!! Mama Leslie - he loved nothin' better than making you laugh! Olivia - well.....picking on you when he slept over – 'nuff said!   2nd family counts for something! David and Leslie - y'all missed the boat cuz now he's gone and M is no longer a minor - might need to change the will!!!!

TO THE WIFE WHO HAS ANXIETY AND DEPRESSION, FROM YOU HUSBAND

To my wife and my best friend,

When we first met five years ago, I never thought I would be writing this. As we stood on stage in front of all of those strangers, acting our hearts out, I never once believed we would find ourselves here. We've come a long way.

When we first met, I'd never been truly close to a person who suffered from long-term anxiety and severe depression. They'd been merely buzzwords thrown around too many times by people who couldn't think of another way to describe their daily frustrations.

"I think I'm going to have a panic attack." or "Oh my gosh, I'm so depressed" became a monotonous phrase that strangers were all too happy to proclaim when the coffee shop ran out of their favorite muffin or they were forced to stay in the library a little later than normal to finish a paper instead of going to the bars with their friends. It was a signal to others they had problems and they wanted people to recognize and sympathize with their petty difficulties.

But you were different. I never saw this monotony in you. To the contrary, you were always so bright and full of life and energy. But then, slowly, I started to see the side of you that you were so apt to hide from me and the rest of the world for fear of being found out.

When you reached your lowest low, it was difficult for me to not take personally your statements asking me to simply let you be and that you needed to work through it on your own. That there was nothing I could do to be a better husband or companion and help your sadness and anxiety go away and that, yes, you were crying, but it was nothing I had done. At that time, I'm sad to say, your assurances fell on deaf ears.

When you reached your lowest low, you said something to me I will never be fully equipped to handle. "The only reason I'm still alive is because I couldn't do that to you. I couldn't kill myself only because I know how much it would hurt you." That's what you said. It broke my heart. In one sweeping statement, you managed to communicate exactly how much you value me and at the same time how much value you have placed on yourself.

The multiple days where you would stay in bed, or not shower, or the days where eating a meal seemed like too much work. The times I would catch you crying and you would try to hide it in a (poor) attempt to smooth everything over.

We have now been together five years and married for nearly two of them. The time we've spent together has been amazing but truly defines an "emotional roller coaster." Writing from the perspective of a husband who always likes to consider himself truly honest and, for lack of a better term, "manly," it seemed inconceivable for me at first that there were days I couldn't make you feel better. That I was powerless to change how you felt.

The frustration that comes with not being able to tell your depressed wife how much you love her, how each day is brighter with her in it, and instead knowing she will simply smile and not fully believe you or not realize what you're trying to communicate is truly one of the hardest feelings I've ever had to overcome. In a word, I felt helpless. Leading up to our wedding and even a few months past it, I felt absolutely immobilized. I firmly believed there was nothing I could do. I felt trapped in a cycle of trying to understand your depression, to getting frustrated when it got too bad, and finally returning to wanting nothing more but to help you feel better. A truly unenviable position for any new husband.

But today is a brighter day. It is more than a one year since that day and, after numerous phone calls and quite a few tears, you have been meeting with a psychologist who has helped you (well... helped both of us) learn to deal with your depression and anxiety in a healthy, controlled way. I have learned that there will always be days when you are down. Days when you are not quite yourself. And, while some days are a struggle, I am still trying to learn that when you are unhappy, there may not be a root cause. I know it still scares you. While your suicidal thoughts have dissipated, I know you constantly think about a day when they might reenter our lives and the home we have made. But know that this time... this time I will be ready. When we first met, I was a foolish college boy with a tremendous crush. I was not properly equipped to handle the effects of mental illness, nor was I ready to deal with the perceived backlash I thought could only be my fault. I was ready to give in to whatever you wanted, even if those tendencies were reckless or self-destructive. Today, I am a man. Today I am your husband. When we first met, I thought you were different. I was right. Because despite the internal battle you fight on a daily basis, you still manage to be truly the best wife I could have ever hoped for. Despite the challenges mental illness will no doubt bring to our future, I welcome them head on. So long as we can do it together.

Your vigilant defender, Your husband.

JUSTICE SERVED!!!!!! ACTIONS HAVE CONSEQUENCES!!!!!!

JUDGE FINDS TEEN GUILTY!!!!

In a case that hinged largely on a teenage couple's intimate text messages, Michelle Carter was found guilty of involuntary manslaughter Friday in the 2014 death of her boyfriend, who poisoned himself by inhaling carbon monoxide in his pickup truck, a Massachusetts judge ruled.

Carter's own words -- preserved in hundreds of text messages presented as evidence over six days of testimony -- helped seal her conviction in the death of 18-year-old Conrad Roy III, Bristol County Juvenile Court Judge Lawrence Moniz said during a 15-minute explanation of his rationale.

"She admits in ... texts that she did nothing: She did not call the police or Mr. Roy's family" after hearing his last breaths during a phone call, Moniz said. "And, finally, she did not issue a simple additional instruction: Get out of the truck."

Carter, 20, cried silently as Moniz spoke. She stood to receive the ruling, which could set legal precedent for whether it's a crime to tell someone to commit suicide.

'There are no winners here'

Prosecutors had argued that Carter sent Roy numerous text messages urging him to commit suicide, listened over the phone as he suffocated and failed to alert authorities or his family that he'd died. The judge agreed. Michelle Carter reacts as the judge explains his rationale for his guilty finding in her manslaughter case.

"This court has found that Carter's actions and failure to act where it was her self-created duty to Roy since she put him in that toxic environment constituted reckless conduct," the judge said. "The court finds that the conduct caused the death of Mr. Roy."

With Carter standing, Moniz said, "This court, having reviewed the evidence, finds you guilty on the indictment with involuntary manslaughter." Although Cater was not present when Roy killed himself, her text messages and conversations with him proved damning.

One July 2012 exchange of texts messages was typical:

Roy: "I'm over thinking"

Carter: "I thought you wanted to do this. The time is right and you're ready, you just need to do it! You can't keep living this way. You just need to do it like you did last time and not think about it and just do it babe. You can't keep doing this everyday."

Roy's relatives, who sat near Carter in the front row of the courtroom, wept as the judge ticked through the steps Roy took to end his life, as well as Carter's complicity. Sitting opposite them, Carter's family members also sobbed.

"Although we are very pleased with the verdict, in reality there are no winners here," prosecutor Katie Rayburn told reporters later.

"Two families had been torn apart and will be affected by this for years to come. We hope verdict will bring some closure... It's been an extremely emotionally draining process for everyone involved."

Texting suicide trial reveals legal shades of gray

Roy aspired to be a tugboat captain and would be alive if not for Carter's actions, Rayburn said. He had been trying to better himself, and "we all wish he had the opportunity" to grow up, she said.

Added Roy's father, Conrad Roy Jr.: "This has been a very tough time for our family, and we would just like to process this verdict that we are happy with." Moniz let Carter, who was tried as a juvenile because she was 17 at the time of the crime, remain free on bail until her sentencing on August 3. She could face up to 20 years in prison, though experts say such a lengthy sentence is unlikely. She was ordered to have no contact with members of the Roy family. She cannot apply for or obtain a passport, nor can she leave Massachusetts without permission from a judge.

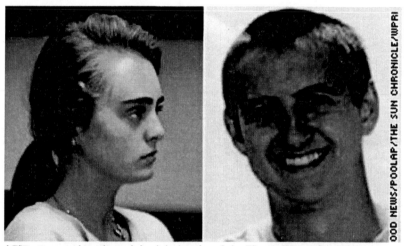

⊠img alt⊠"Texting suicide trial reveals legal shades of gray" class⊠"media⊠image" src⊠"//i2.cdn.cnn.com/cnnnext/dam/assets/170610114404-michelle-carter-conrad-roy-split-large-169.jpg"⊠

Case was watched closely. The ruling, which may spur lawmakers to codify the behavior highlighted in the case as criminal, was closely watched by legal experts.

"Given the expansive definition of manslaughter under Massachusetts law, the guilty verdict is not a surprise," CNN legal analyst Danny Cevallos said. "Still, this verdict is concerning because it reflects a judicial willingness to expand legal liability for another person's suicide, an act which by definition is a completely independent choice," he said. "Historically, suicide has been considered a superseding act which breaks the chain of legal causation."

In charging Carter with involuntary manslaughter, prosecutors were threading a legal needle, another legal expert said.

"I thought it was a square peg in a round hole, it wasn't a great fit for manslaughter," Daniel Medwed, professor of law and criminal justice at Northeastern University, said after the decision. "Her behavior was so morally reprehensible, but I wasn't sure how, as a matter of law, it constituted as manslaughter."

Medwed said manslaughter involves direct action such as a drunk driver who slams into a car or someone who fires a gun into a crowd to recklessly cause a death.

"This case involves mainly words, but ultimately ⊠Roy⊠decided to do the deed, so it didn't fit in with the classic pattern of manslaughter," he said. "But the facts are so powerful, so compelling and her behavior so apparent that I'm not shocked she got convicted for manslaughter."

Texts drove suicide, prosecutors argued.

Carter secretly nudged Roy toward suicide by sending him numerous text messages encouraging him to take his life, prosecutors said. In closing arguments Tuesday, prosecutors said Carter berated her vulnerable boyfriend when he had second thoughts about killing himself, listened by phone as he died and used his suicide to get from friends the attention that she desperately craved.

Teens and Texts:

Suicide case exposes risks of messaging Carter went from offering "words of kindness and love" to aggressively encouraging Roy via text message to carry out longtime threats to commit suicide, Rayburn told the court.

"It got to the point that he was apologizing to her, ... apologizing to her for not being dead yet," she said in her closing argument.

Rayburn reminded the judge of text messages in which Carter encouraged Roy to get back in the truck. In text messages to a friend, she described hearing his final words and breaths on the phone.

Roy's body was found July 13, 2014, a day after his suicide in his parked truck in a Kmart parking lot in Fairhaven, nearly 40 miles from his home.

'Tragic ... not a homicide,' defense said

Carter's attorney argued she was a troubled, delusional young woman who was "dragged" into the suicidal journey of Roy, who had long been intent on killing himself.

Assistance or coercion?

Intent is key in text message suicide case, experts say "The evidence actually established that Conrad Roy caused his own death by his physical actions and by his own thoughts," defense attorney Joseph Cataldo said. "You're dealing with an individual who wanted to take his own life. ... He dragged Michelle Carter into this."

Carter was "overwhelmed" by Roy's talk of suicide while at the same time dealing "with all of her baggage," including the side effects of medication for depression, Cataldo said.

"It's sad, it's tragic," he said. "It's just not a homicide."

Earlier in the trial, a psychiatrist testified that Carter was delusional after becoming "involuntarily intoxicated" by antidepressants. She was "unable to form intent" after switching to a new, prescription drug months before Roy's suicide, and she even texted his phone for weeks after he died, the psychiatrist testified. Follow @RaySanchezNYC CNN's Michelle Krupa, Jessica Suerth, Sarah Jorgensen and Darran Simon contributed to this report.

Day 8 of Thankfulness Challenge:
Daddy, or otherwise known as Mr. Morgan, counselor at SHS:
Both of my kids were named after him - she, Morgan and Pierce
had his first name Bobby. If it wasn't for Daddy wanting a girl,
filling out the paper work, filing it with the courts, and the
Methodist Home in San Antonio, to adopt a girl, he wouldn't
have been my dad. He set an example, through quiet observing
ways, of how to be a man, serve your family, put family first, give
advice when you weren't even aware he was paying attention, to
love unconditionally, and showed me the type man I should
marry; thus, Timbo. This photo was taken at his 70th birthday
party with Morgan.

On Father's Day, Tim got us tickets to see the movie Megan Kelly,
which is about a female Marine who becomes a dog handler in the
Afgan war and fights to eventually bring the retired dog home with
her. The movie didn't start until six, but he didn't want to sit
around the house, so we went to lunch and then to a patio bar
before the movie. I could tell he was upset, having to do Father's
Day without Pierce.
I shared the following memory:

bobbypierce22   52w

♥ 44 likes

bobbypierce22 Happy father's day I love you dad

Day 9 of Thankfulness Challenge:
Angela, my best friend since 6th grade

Morgan is named after her with her middle name Kay. Although she does not participate in social media, her daughter does and will show her this. I can't imagine going through my life without her. We may not see each other often, but we're the first to run to each other in need. Anytime we are together, it's as if no time has passed at all. Since I only grew up with brothers, she is my version of a sister. She's the type person that if you called her in the middle of the night, said you were broken down in South Dakota, she'd say, 'ok, I'm on my way.' She is a fantastic mom; terrific aunt; loving wife; loyal daughter; excellent dental hygienist; and friend to many. The saying of 'never met a stranger' definitely applies to her.

When Tim and I first started dating, she went out with us most nights. Our regular spot, Bennigan's on Hulen, the bar tender never knew which one of us was dating Tim. And he was always amused that Tim could keep up with our ever changing conversations! So thankful she's my person!

From the page 'Depression Kills':
Little boy: Are you an angel?
Me: What?
Little boy: My mum told me those who have marked wrist are angels.
Me: I'm not an angel.
Little boy: Of course you are. Mum said that only angels harm themselves because they don't like life on earth. This world is destroying them so they try to return to heaven again. They are too sensitive to the pain of others and their own.
Me: You know your mum is very wise.
Little boy: Thank you. She's also an angel but she has already returned home.

Anxiety, Depression and College
I survived, and actually thrived, in college despite mental health disorders, and so can you.
By Brittany Sodic, University of North Texas
Four years of full-time classes and part-time work is hard for any student. For students living with mental health disorders, everyday challenges related to their conditions only add to the general stress of school. I struggled with extreme anxiety and depression throughout the entirety of my college career, and sometimes it was too much to endure. But, I ended up graduating Cum Laude, scored an awesome internship and found myself succeeding in everything I attempted, despite my disorders. There was a bit of trial and error when figuring out how to reconcile my drive to succeed with the constant drag of my mental state. Here are the main lessons I've learned during that period that might be helpful to other students.

1.   **Talk**
Talk to someone about what you are going through mentally and emotionally. Talk to a pet. Talk to yourself out loud at first, if that's where you find to start. It doesn't matter who you talk to, as long as you're actively talking and getting
The most important thing is to talk to someone that you trust, but if you are talking to a professional counselor or therapist, even better.

Figure out what is troubling you. You need to figuring out how to reconcile my drive to succeed with the constant drag of my mental state. Many universities and colleges offer mental health resources, such as counseling, for their students. Unfortunately, these resources are often vastly underused; either because of the stigma of seeking help for mental health disorders, or because students don't know where to look for them. My university offered a set number of free counseling sessions per semester, and I regret not taking advantage of those services more when I needed them.

Find out if your school offers counseling or mental health programs for students and, most importantly, don't be afraid to show up once you do find them.

2.   **Moderate Your Alcohol Consumption**

Okay, you're in college; this one is hard, I know. No matter your friend group is, activities you're involved in or even your age, alcohol is going to be involved in your life during your time in school. My advice for those suffering from a mental health disorder, like I did: Use alcohol sparingly, if at all. Have fun, but don't turn to alcohol when you're not in the right mindset to enjoy it.

It's easy to convince yourself that you need to "go out" and have fun with your friends when you're anxious and want a distraction from the onslaught of worries in your own mind, or if you're feeling down and need a "pick-me-up." But, in my experience, drinking will only make you feel worse about yourself in the long run. Anxiety forces me to replay everything I said or did the night before, even if I did nothing objectively embarrassing, and I will surely spiral into shame, guilt and self-criticism of an abnormal intensity. The day-after-drinking anxiety spiral just contributes further to whatever I was trying to run from in the first place, be it my anxiety or depression. Wait until you're drinking for the right reasons—to celebrate or enjoy yourself, and only when you're feeling well and positive. This will undoubtedly result in you missing some social events in order to practice self-care.

3.   **Curb Your FOMO**

At certain points throughout school, I was so depressed and reluctant to have human contact that I would not leave my apartment for days at a time. If I did leave, I would return to my sanctuary as fast as possible. During these periods of self-imposed isolation, I would get on social media and see all of the friends that I was unintentionally avoiding having a great time in their photos and posts. I felt like I was missing out on the "college experience," whatever that actually means. On the other end of the spectrum, when I was not in a depressive episode and willing and wanting to go out, sometimes my anxiety was so great that I had to stay in to take care of myself.

I knew crowds, loud music and unfamiliarity would only exacerbate the feelings I was having. Passing on lunch or movie plans with friends became a common occurrence.

College is full of experiences though, and I realized that I don't need to have all of them. Four years is a long time to cultivate friendships and memorable moments, anyway. So don't be afraid to take a day or two off to focus on yourself if you need it, as long as it doesn't negatively affect your school or work. And don't be afraid of missing anything; you're more important.

4.   **Be Open with Others**

It took me awhile to learn that people will be more understanding, caring and patient if you explain that you're struggling with a mental-health disorder. This new policy of mine to try and be up front and honest about the struggle with my disorders has improved my relationships with friends, coworkers and professors. Explain to your friends why you need to cancel those plans, or why you've been distant or seemingly irritable with them. Once you do, they'll realize that they shouldn't take it personally if you're feeling off, and will most likely want to do everything they can to help you. You may find, like I did, that some of your friends have similar disorders and can take solace in the camaraderie of that commonality. Engaging in conversations with my professors about why I needed to leave the classroom when I was having a panic attack, or why I was struggling to focus on a certain assignment, strengthened our student-teacher relationship. Had I not been honest with my instructors, I know that my grades would have suffered in participation points or quizzes missed when I was unable to stave off a panic attack during class. They helped me when I needed it, and you'll probably find your professors to be as helpful if you let them know what's wrong.

5.   **Find Your Passion and Pursue It**

For a few years, I've used yoga as a way to rehabilitate myself from trauma, pull myself out of depression and quell the anxious thoughts in my head. Yoga helped me connect to myself again, gave me an outlet for negative vibes and also equipped me with useful techniques, such as slow and controlled breathing, to help with my anxiety.

Yoga isn't for everyone, but you can find your equivalent in anything you love to do. If you don't know what your "thing" is, don't worry. College is a great place to sample different interests and find what works for you. Even better, most of it is free. Write, make music, play intramural sports, volunteer, get into photography, join a club. Just do something, and then put your heart and love behind it. Whatever you choose to pursue will return the love tenfold with positive change for your mental wellness.

5. **Nobody Knows You Better Than You**

Remember that everybody is different and requires individualized care. My experience may not be totally applicable to your situation, and that's okay. Just try to find what works for you, and stick with it. You got this.

I received this message:

Bobbi, we have never met and I did not know your son, but I wanted to say something to you. I don't have any appropriate words. I don't have any frame of reference. I lost my brother too soon but it was a different story. I almost lost my son to a stroke and he survived. I have known some grief, but nothing like the burden you must carry. I am humbled, inspired, and broken by your posts. I cannot imagine the unthinkable grief that you have endured. I cannot imagine the loss and the daily struggle. I just want to say that it is an honor to pray for your family as you are allowing others to see a glimpse of how you are coping and using your sorrow for good. My prayer for you and your family is that you will always be uplifted, that you will feel the peace the surpasses understanding that can only come from our loving Father. Praying for your husband tomorrow as I can imagine it is another difficult day for him. Thank you for sharing your story. Thank you for allowing others to see. Thank you for your effort to raise awareness. I have no doubt that lives will be saved and forever changed because you are sharing.

–Amy, Allen, Tx

It means so much to me when people reach out to me and lend their support of my efforts! What an incredible blessing!

Sometimes it's too late to make things right. Sometimes we hurt others more than we realize. Sometimes a smile fades in front of our eyes, and sometimes, we are the reason for tears in someone's eyes. Never treat anyone the way you don't want to be treated. Love life and love the ones around you. Type Yes if you agree.
WomenWorking.com

Article from the Red Ledger of Lovejoy HS:
Nathalie Kroll, Staff Reporter
April 17, 2013

While walking down the hall on April 16, many students may have been caught off guard by the amount of students with a semicolon on their wrists. Taking part in the Semicolon Project, the day was designed to raise awareness for those with anxiety, depression, or even thoughts of suicide. "I drew a semicolon on my wrist in order to symbolize that I'm the author of my own life; I'm in complete control of my life, I dictate it, and I have the ultimate choice in deciding how I want my story to play out," junior Heloise Rytzell said. "I'm not only doing this for myself, but everyone else out there who struggles with depression, self-harm, unhappiness, a broken heart, anxiety, etc." The story behind the semicolon, is that in English literature, a semicolon is used where an author could have decided to end the sentence, but instead let the sentence run on. This is used as a metaphor for life, where one, who is the author of their own life, could have decided to end their own life, but instead decided to keep going. "What I love about the Semicolon Project is that it has the potential to bring people, who wouldn't normally talk, together," junior Kassidy Cox said. "So many people have been through things that not everyone knows about, and I applaud people who have semicolons on their wrists because that is so strong and honest of them." Although some students who do struggle with depression and anxiety had semicolons on their wrists, many students who don't struggle a mood disorder supported the cause as well. "Everybody has their own situations, and people need somebody to know that there's somebody who always cares for them no matter what," junior Ryan Block said, "I think it's good for people to know that I'm always there for somebody, no matter who, and their situation." The students that took part in the Semicolon Project feel that it is important to show unity and to comfort those who do struggle with problems that would not otherwise be brought to light. "It is a great way to show your support to others who are going through hard times in life, and it represents that you are ultimately in charge of your own life, so the sentence – life – doesn't have to end where it should," junior Allie Carrell said. "So even if you feel like there's no way out, you can extend your life story by extending the sentence."

The Semicolon Project not only affects students on campus, but it is a nationwide project that is trying to bring to light the struggles many people, especially teenagers, face.

April is both the Stress Awareness Month and Self Harm Awareness month, which can both be supported by an orange ribbon. "I think that the project is a really amazing thing where you see that you're not alone in the things that you may struggle with," junior Jenna Reitinger said.

"By putting a semicolon on your wrist it is making a promise to yourself that it is okay to seek help and show that you're a strong person."

DAY 10 THANKFULNESS CHALLENGE:
My in-laws, Bill & Pat Gilbert.

They raised three headstrong young men who all grew up to be great husbands and dads. They are one of the best examples of true, good Christians; not just on Sunday's at church, but every day. They set the example for me on forgiveness by forgiving for the sake of family; which, led me to be able to forgive Sarah. Forgiveness is the one commandments most Christian's struggle with the most. They strive to attend all family get-togethers and their grandkids activities. They visit family in Louisiana and have recently moved back to the hill country & love living in a retirement community.

'You tell me that your sorry,
didn't think I'd turn around,
and say,
It's too late to apologize
it's too late
I said it's too late to apologize
It's too late'
'Apologize' - One Republic

July 2017

Karli came to see me!!!! She was home for a month after moving overseas to finish her college degree! She is doing great! She is in such a good place in her life and is genially happy!!!!!! Seeing her again, being in her presence, truly made me over the moon happy!!!!!! I cannot begin to express how wonderful it was to see her again. She was my 'late night counselor' after P's choice of April 20th. She clung to me; rather than, run from me, as so many did after. I honestly don't know where I'd be in my journey without God blessing me with her through the first year. She will forever and always hold a special place in my heart! We all love her like family! I cannot wait to see what the future holds for her!

Article from the Red Ledger Lovejoy HS:
Ignorance is bliss, but not for the ignored
The Red Ledger Staff
September 22, 2015
Though last week was not as publicized as Breast Cancer Awareness Month or even a school's Red Ribbon Week, it was just as important as any. Monday, Sept. 7, marked the start of National Suicide Prevention Week and Thursday, Sept. 10, is recognized as as World Suicide Prevention Day. While it may be uncomfortable, talking about suicide is a vitally important step to preventing suicide.
Publicizing it to gain support and end social stigmas around suicide is the first step to preventing it as a whole.

It's not surprising that reading this article may be the first time that you're hearing of this. The lack of publicity given to the topic of suicide stems from the fact that people tend to not want to talk about things that are unpleasant, because it's easier to just pretend that suicide does not take a life roughly every 40 seconds. It's easier to ignore the fact that suicide is the cause of death for 800,000 people per year. However, while it is so easy to ignore the dark parts of life that could be silently affecting anyone around us, it is important to recognize that mental disorders affect many people around us without us knowing, and they are very real.

A common misconception regarding mental illness involves just how common these illnesses are. In fact, suicide was the second leading cause of death in people 15-29 years old during 2013 and 1 in 12 teens have engaged in self-harming activities. When people read statistics like these, they read them as numbers that are valid, but that only affect people outside of their family, their school, or their community. It is not easy to think about how these things happen to people that we interact with every day.

In order to prevent suicide and find new and more effective treatments for mental disorders than can lead to suicide, we, as a society, must publicize it. Despite the misconception that talking about suicide will "put the thought in someone's head," increasing the public awareness of the reality of suicide will aid in ending the stereotypes that are actually harmful to potential victims, and talking to someone about this subject is not going to be the deciding factor of whether or not they become suicidal.

As current chair of the American Association of Suicidology Julie Cerel Ph.D said in an article on Healthline News , open discussion about a disease can make all the difference.

"In the 1970s, you would never go to the grocery store and talk about cancer, or talk about breasts. Neither one of those were topics we talked about publicly," she said.

"And now you can't avoid a store that isn't pink for breast cancer awareness, which is wonderful. And the number of breast cancer deaths have declined so dramatically." The publicity given to breast cancer has led to millions of dollars donated for research and millions of lives saved worldwide. Talking about suicide is not going to end it, the same way that talking about breast cancer doesn't shrink malignant tumors. However, publicizing suicide can aid in raising the money and public awareness necessary to end suicide as a whole.

Day 11 THANKFULNESS CHALLENGE:
My Mama:

The best seamstress of all time. Maker of: the kids smocked clothes; Pierce's rag-quilt; my wedding gown; tea kettle cozies, quilts, stockings, etc. She is the one everyone catches up with the most often; thus, she can keep you up to date on everyone else's life. She makes the best dressing for Thanksgiving and Christmas. She's a fabulous GanMom & MeeMaw! If I ever have a question about something, she is who I call first and she 99⬚ of the time can give me an answer. She modeled for me how to be a good mom & God couldn't have blessed me with a better one than her!

P with his favorite teacher Mrs. Saffle from Hart Elementary. They both shared the same sense of humor and she taught him in both 4th & 5th grade.

This article was written by a former neighbor of ours:

Former staff member Jordan Toomey chose to get a semi-colon tattoo on her wrist where she once self-harmed. The tattoo symbolizes the fact that she chose to pause her story, not to end it.

Editor's note: The week of Sept. 5-11 is National Suicide Prevention Week. In observance of the week, The Red Ledger asked former staff member and 2016 graduate Jordan Toomey to share her journey through depression and suicidal thoughts.

I'm sitting in my economics classroom my senior year, at my desk, arms wrapped around myself to keep from shaking as the presentation begins. A woman with an annoyingly calm voice slowly flicks through slides about signs a person may be considering suicide, how to help, and, in the same neutral voice, urges us to think before we act. One of my classmates cracks a joke in the back of the room, and most of the class laughs. Even the presenter smiles indulgently.

I touch the still-healing cuts on my wrists, hidden by my oversized plaid shirt, and cast my eyes downward.

I am not laughing.

The school can pay someone to come and spit facts at high schoolers about depression, self-harming behaviors, and suicide, but that doesn't mean that they can make the kids listen.

The worst part is, I don't even blame them f̶
eyed woman rattling off facts that she obviousl̶
and most of the class, suicide is something they do̶
It's something that most people don't have to worry a̶
most people don't know is happening. Except that's not t̶
statistics, 117 people die per day from suicide. It is thought t̶
teens self-harm.

I am no exception.

"Someone telling the school counselor about my self-harm may have sa̶
my life. "— Jordan Toomey

I first really learned what depression was the first semester of my junior
year, while working on a collaborative story about mental illness for The
Red Ledger. While learning what it really was, and asking my friend who
had been diagnosed with it personal questions about his experiences, I
began to feel something: relief. Finally, I had a word to describe the sinking
feeling I had been experiencing for the last few months. I had a word to
describe the excessive crying, the lack of motivation, the loss of energy, the
isolation from friends, and the intense pain I sometimes felt in my chest. I
had depression. With this realization, my brain rebelled. Sure, I was
depressed...but it couldn't be that bad. I was just overreacting. I pushed it
to the side, unwilling to deal with it. I waited for it to get better.

It didn't.

My grades dropped, friendships failed, and I became suicidal. The
beginning of my senior year, I started self-harming. The small cuts quickly
morphed into a full-blown addiction, and it got so bad that I cut almost
every night for two months straight. I wore a leather jacket over my
birthday dress to hide the cuts. I was scared to push my sleeves up, even if
it got warm in the classroom. I cried every night, and hoped for death. I
came to school with eyes so lifeless that teachers I had never even met went
out of their way to ask if I was okay. I didn't talk to my friends very often,
and it came to a point where I really didn't have any.

This is what depression does to you. This is what self-harm does to you.
This is my story, and it is real. I roamed the hallways with everyone who is
reading this article.

I might have stood next to you in the lunch line.

I might have sat next to you in class.

I might have been one of your closest friends or one of your worst
enemies. And I almost killed myself.

as come to my attention
t it. One of my friends
as "contagious." This
)ecause I can dangle
"look for," but the
feet under right now.
vning, and you probably

y're OK. I'm not
st chance you get, but
ut my self-harm may

r not listening to this dull-
doesn't care about. To her,
't have to worry about.
out, something
rue. By latest
hat 1 in 12
ved

This week is dedicated to suicide prevention, and it is not a joke.
It is not some monotonous message like "be nice to each other,"
that we learned in preschool. Suicide prevention and awareness
week is so incredibly important for people out there who are
contemplating taking their own lives. Losing a life to a chemical
imbalance in the brain, to bullying, to inability to cope with
anxiety or OCD or PTSD – this is a big deal. It should be treated
as a big deal.

To anyone out there who struggles with mental illness, self-harm,
or suicidal thoughts – I am with you. Take medication, draw little
pictures on the areas of your body where you cut (I personally got
a tattoo where I used to cut), and remind yourself that: It. Gets.
Better. Because it does.

If you are someone who does not have a mental illness, does not
self-harm, and does not consider killing themselves – good. But
please be aware that there are people around you who are
struggling with these things. They need help. They need love. And
above everything else, they need you to know what's happening in
the world and what's happening in their heads. And that's what
suicide prevention week is about; making the general populace
aware of a silent war happening in people's minds.

If things had been even a little different, my seat at the front of my
economics room would have been cold, empty. The woman
would have droned on and on about how it was important to
watch people for signs of self-harm, depression, and suicide.
And no one would have been laughing.

For the National Suicide Prevention Lifeline, call 1-800-273-8255.

TBT to Pierce's first dirt bike and when he was in his flip-flop phase.

It's time to recognize mental health as essential to physical health
By JOHN CAMPO MAY 31, 2017

The human brain is a wonder. Through folds of tissue and pulses of electricity, it lets us perceive, attempt to understand, and shape the world around us. As science rapidly charts the brain's complex structures, new discoveries are revealing the biology of how the mind functions and fails. Given the centrality of the brain to human health, its malfunctions should be a priority, separated from stigma and treated on par with the diseases of the body. We aren't there yet, but the transformation is underway.

Mental disorders affect nearly 20 percent of American adults; nearly 4 percent are severely impaired and classified as having serious mental illness. These disorders are often associated with chronic physical illnesses such as heart disease and diabetes. They also increase the risk of physical injury and death through accidents, violence, and suicide.

Suicide alone was responsible for 42,773 deaths in the United States in 2014 (the last year for which final data are available), making it the 10th leading cause of death. Among adolescents and young adults, suicide is responsible for more deaths than the combination of cancer, heart disease, congenital anomalies, respiratory disease, influenza, pneumonia, stroke, meningitis, septicemia, HIV, diabetes, anemia, and kidney and liver disease.

The treatment of mental illness has long been held back by the sense that disorders of emotion, thinking, and behavior somehow lack legitimacy and instead reflect individual weakness or poor life choices. Not surprisingly, there has been a mismatch between the enormous impact of mental illness and addiction on the public's health and our society's limited commitment to addressing these problems.

Here are three examples of how that plays out:

Most emergency departments are ill-equipped to meet the needs of patients in the midst of mental health crises.

Most insurance plans view mental illness and addiction as exceptions to standard care, not part of it.

Despite an overall cultural shift towards compassion, our society still tends to view the mentally ill and those with addiction as morally broken rather than as ill. Your mind can be trained to control chronic pain. But it will cost you Too often, individuals suffering from serious mental illnesses — those in greatest need of care — have been isolated and cared for outside of traditional health care, as in the asylums of the past. There, mental health care was separate from, and far from equal to, traditional health care. Why the disconnect? Psychiatry has been hampered by an inability to observe and record the physical workings of the brain. Because of that, psychiatric assessments and treatments have been viewed as somewhat mysterious. Even today, the underlying mechanisms behind some of the most powerful and effective psychiatric treatments are still poorly understood. All of that translates into the difficulty that many people have finding help for real, disabling symptoms attributed to a mental illness or addiction. However, just as other fields of medicine have evolved as knowledge advanced during the past century, psychiatry has also made profound gains. Advances emerging from unlocking the brain's physiology and biochemistry are coming at a time when mental health care is being integrated into traditional health care. The potential has never been greater to finally bring psychiatry quite literally under the same roof as the rest of medicine.

The Ohio State University Wexner Medical Center, where I work, offers an example of this kind of transformation. Now celebrating its centenary, the Ohio State Harding Hospital was founded as the Indianola Rest Home by Dr. George Harding II, younger brother of President Warren G. Harding. It was created as an asylum that provided quiet, nutrition, and a focus on spirituality.

Today, the hospital can address mental health issues as effectively as it treats trauma or cardiac arrest. This shift is occurring nationally, with community-involved, comprehensive mental health integration into hospitals in cities and rural communities alike.

Psychiatric drugs haven't improved for decades. So researchers are scouring the brain for leads.

Proven regimens for treating common mental disorders and addictions are aiding the "cure" rate and boosting public acceptance that such care works. Modern practices have the potential to improve public health and, perhaps equally important, engage families more actively in the care of individuals suffering from mental disorders and addictions.

I find it fascinating to see the commonsense approaches to treating mental illness once employed by the Indianola Rest Home increasingly being accepted within mainstream medicine. Bringing together the sensibilities and experience of the past with state-of-the-art modern medicine often makes good sense.

Will the stigma of mental illness finally fade? Better understanding of the human brain and the biological nature of the mind will help, but it won't be enough. How we think about mental health matters. When mental health is ultimately recognized as essential to physical health, not an extraneous element of it, then we will have access to true, complete, modern medicine. - John V. Campo, MD, is professor and chair of the Department of Psychiatry and Behavioral Health at The Ohio State University Wexner Medical Center in Columbus, Ohio.

Brutally Honest Post Explains How Girls Are Abusing Their Boyfriends, Check If You're Not Doing It Too

We usually think of abusive relationships as black eyes and broken noses; but, abuse isn't limited to physical traumas. Psychological scars can be just as – if not more – painful and, sadly, any relationship can inflict them, even if you're dating a teen girl.

Signs of an abusive relationship, however, is sometimes hard to spot; even, for a professional.

Boy may not realize they are the victims. Especially if they're madly in love. That's why someone posted an honest message on Tumblr which should help identify if a teen girl is abusing her partner. The post quickly gained attention and so far it has amassed almost 290k notes.

People are even re-blogging it in spite of losing followers. Scroll down to read the brilliant text, and let's hope more people will openly discuss this uncomfortable yet very important topic.

Dear teen girls,
STOP ABUSING YOUR BOYFRIENDS AND YES WHAT YOU ARE DOING IS ABUSE:

STOP:
Yelling at him in front of his friends
Hitting or slapping him when he does or says something you don't like
Telling him he doesn't have a choice when it comes to decisions that involve both of you
Telling him he can't hang out with friends because you don't like them
Telling him not to talk to other girls even if they are his friends
Forcing him to spend every moment with you
Belittling him and pointing out flaws
Calling him stupid or making fun of making mistakes
Threatening to break up with him if he doesn't do what you want
Being emotionally manipulative and crying until he does what you want
Accusing him of cheating on you every time he's not with you

Blow up his phone if he doesn't text you back in five minutes

Telling him you are the best thing that has ever happened to him and no one else will love him

Physically attacking him whenever you are mad

Forcing him to have sex despite the fact that he said he didn't want to

Invading his privacy by going through his phone

Getting mad at him for changing his password and demanding he tell you what it is

If a guy did ANY of these things to a girl, it would be considered abuse; but, since it's the other way around, it's considered normal. Today, so many high school girls are treating their boyfriends like shit. Even sometimes physically abusing them in the hallway and no one trying to stop it because it's a girl attacking a boy.

BOYS: if your girlfriend does anything on this list, leave her. It is abuse and you deserve better!

GIRLS: if you find yourself doing anything on this list to your boyfriend, you need to knock it off because you are being abusive!
-taken from BordedPanda site

UGH!!!!!!! THIS SO DESCRIBES SARAH – TO A TEE!!!!!!!!

I wish I had realized all the games, manipulations, and level of stress she was heaping on him. No wonder he couldn't handle it anymore! It explains his anxiety levels being though the roof and it all boiling over into his anger that led to his depression.

The Strongest Girls Are The Girls With Anxiety

- Holly Riordan

She's strong, because she's in a constant battle with her anxiety. It's telling her that she's weak. That she shouldn't speak up. That she shouldn't get out of bed. Some days, she listens to everything that voice tells her.

But other days, she finds the power to ignore it. She finds the strength to leave her room. To socialize. To smile.

She's strong, because she shows up, even when she's shaking. She speaks, even when it's with a cracked voice. She keeps breathing, even when those breaths are shaky.

It would be easy for her to cancel plans with her friends, turn down dates, skip class, call in sick from work — and sometimes, she does.

Sometimes, the idea of being around people is too much for her to handle. But most of the time, she does what she has to do. She switches off her alarm. She showers. She dresses. And then she gets shit done.

Of course, she gets distracted throughout the day. The tiniest thing can send her mind spinning. A text from someone she didn't expect to hear from. An email she isn't quite sure how to answer. A strange look from one of her coworkers or crushes.

She suffers from constant self-consciousness, but she pushes past it. She ignores the way she thinks everyone is looking at her, judging her, and she forces herself to be productive. She forces herself to focus on what's important.

She refuses to let anxiety control her life. She won't let her dark thoughts eclipse the positive ones. She's motivated to be the best person she can be.

At times, her anxiety makes her feel weak. Lesser. Like she doesn't deserve to be in the same room as people that can talk to strangers as if they've known each other for years.

But even though she feels inferior, that's far from the truth. She's a warrior. A bad-ass. Why can't she see that? She tries so hard. She puts in so much effort. And she's gotten so far.

Some people rarely venture outside of their comfort zone — but she's outside of her comfort zone every damn day. She's either worried about what to say or what to wear or where to park. She's never relaxed. She's always on edge. That's why she's always learning. Always growing. Every second of every day.

Sure, there are times when she suffers from setbacks. When she doesn't say a single word for hours. When she stays in her pajamas and puts off showering. But there are other times when she finds the courage to speak her mind.

When she surprises herself with how brave she can be. She probably doesn't realize it yet, but girls with anxiety are the strongest girls in the world, because they never have a minute of peace. Because they're always struggling — and they're always winning.

Day 19 of Thankfulness Challenge:
Jade

She unknowingly became an advocate for suicide awareness this year after the school did not allow my book to be in the library. She handed out books to students and told them to pass it on after they read it. She was a great friend of Pierce & they would ride her four wheeler together here at the ranch. She is a kind, loving, compassionate, caring, giving, and great young lady! We're blessed to have her in our life!

Most women say there is no greater pain
than to bear a child.
I say there is no greater pain
than to bury one.

Day 21 of Thankfulness Challenge:
Tiana

She is the one, the one P should have ended up with; but unfortunately, Sarah found out about her and ruined it! They met when she worked in the neighboring town of ours and at first, were just friends. They shared similar stories of their ex's and planned on dating when she turned 18 (since her parents would not let her date until then). But 2 weeks prior to her b-day, P totally cut her off - all social media, blocked her, etc. and she didn't know why. She found out later he had gotten back with Sarah and she told him he was pathetic for doing so. She never heard from him again (not knowing he was in a mental health hospital and on our lock down after).

The day he committed suicide, her best friend, Gary Zimmer approached her; during passing periods, crying and breaking the news. She refused to believe him and texted Clay, who confirmed the news. She went into class, crying, and the teacher told her to go to the bathroom, rinse off her face, collect herself, and return; instead, she went to the cafeteria and screamed at the top of her lungs, bawling, crying, and not wanting, not able to conceive, Bobby would have done this & that he was actually gone. She reached out to me a few months ago, telling me she knew my son and wasn't sure if I knew who she was or not. I told her yes, I knew of her, but not her name, since his passing, I have a horrible memory. She and I have become good friends since. She finds pennies and dimes all over the place now.

Around mid-June, I started feeling depression settling back in and couldn't figure out why. I fought it for a few weeks; but, it wasn't getting better and I was often weepy. After praying one morning and then running errands, it dawned on me what was going on. It's the ranch. Pierce loved it here and made so many great memories here; but, it's also tainted now since Sarah had spent time here. In all honesty, it hasn't been the same for us since his passing. When we re-did his room, I added my desk in there; yet, I never use it. I always bring my laptop downstairs to do my work on the kitchen table. One day, Tim asked me why. I told him I just can't do my work in his room.

If it was in Morgan's room, that'd be fine; but, just not his room. I am constantly smacked in the face being surrounded by all the memories. I realize not being here won't change the memories; but, it will help to start fresh somewhere new. Also, for Morgan, who often says she doesn't like being here because 'our house feels empty,' a new house would be better.

So, Tim and discussed it and we agreed to selling the ranch. The plan is to rent while we find a new ranch and build a different house. The floor plan is actually the one we had originally planned on building here.

My aunt's text in response to our decision:

Dear Danice & Tim,
I can only imagine how hard it was to make the decision to leave the beautiful house and acreage that you love. This move is no doubt, another step toward healing and taking care of yourselves.

You once told me Danice, how much you admired my strength and courage. I've never experienced anything even close to what you have endured these last two years. But I want you to know, that I; likewise, admire you for your tenacity, your strength, your courage and your desire to help others that have had to endure a loss due to suicide.

I once asked Granny how she managed to get through the death of her daughter, our sister, Jane Ann, to Polio. She said that it was a paralyzing sadness; but one day, a sense of peace just came over her, and after that, she was able to feel a level of acceptance that she had not felt before.

No matter where you choose to live, take care of yourself and continue to move toward your peace. Those of us that love you are cheering you on and praying that the days of dark clouds will become less and that the days with happiness will out- number the sadness.
My sincere love, Jerri

I found this while cleaning out the house, getting it ready to sell.
Yep! He's too cute to be forgotten!

I think it's day 22 of Thankfulness Challenge:
(forgive me if it's a miss step)
LaKeshia:
She loves to claim that I; through my postings, saved her. What she doesn't get, is that - she actually saved me and my advocacy.......
Now, due to us raising our kids in in Collin County and often taking them down to South Dallas; they fully understood what this meant, in terms of where he came from was rough. While I love Whitewright, in terms of small towns; there is, unfortunately, the 'old-timers' who are not open to accepting outsiders. So, even though I did not have to, I made it abundantly clear, that no matter what, my kids would welcome him and stand up for him. Of course Pierce did; because, his 'ten-foot-tall and bullet proof' kicked in! Morgan, being the ever loving sweet heart, often gave him rides home from school. Morgan had been bullied on and off since middle school; so, obviously, she's going to befriend the one treated as an outsider.
On the day when Pierce took his own life, by the time kids had shortly been in school, word/rumors were already beginning to spread. Trolan heard the news and called his Aunt Keshia; crying, demanding she come get him, that he just could not be there! Now, Trolan was not a kid to miss or skip school, so Keshia was puzzled as to why he was so upset that she needed to come get him. When he explained, she said 'I'm on my way!'
After, she started following my page and months later, finally reached out to me. She did not explain our connection to her nephew Trolan; just saying, how much she has struggled in her life, considered suicide, etc. But once she read my post; she knew, no matter what, she could survive anything life threw at her and thanked me for saving her life! I have always said, that if my book can save just one life, then I consider it a success! Thank you LaKeshia, for sustaining me......when I was down in my efforts....for being an answered prayer in my life...for letting me know my efforts are working and that they matter!

I am blessed to count you, you lovely partner, girls and nephew as friends! Now, realizing after the fact, we gave the Mrs. Sadler Culinary Arts Scholarship, to Trolan, all of this, all along, was all Pierce's doing from Heaven above!! #GodIsGreatAllTheTime #TeamPierce

Mid July, I met Kristi, Abigail's mom. Abigail was one of the two teens killed in a horrific accident on Hwy 121 last month (the one previously mentioned in the book). I reached out to her, knowing the path she was about to walk down. Since Pierce's choice of that night, having others who have previously experienced this path reach out to us – has proven to be a HUGE blessing; so, I now feel it's my calling/duty to do the same.

We are forever bonded by what we all wish we were not - the loss of a child. It's the club NO ONE asked to join, NO ONE wants to attend the meetings, NO ONE will pay the dues; yet, here we are, joined together, and it just happens to be a GREAT group of people! It is shockingly amazing to me; still, to this day, the way all this plays out.....the connections that are there; even though, previously, you were unaware.

I felt like I had died too
and they just forgot
to bury me.

Kristi (who works at the Collin County Sheriff's Office) shared with me the stories she has been told since her daughters passing:

In the other vehicle, was a mom, 8 months pregnant, her 4 yr. old, and her parents. The parents died at the scene; the mom was transported via Care Flight, and the baby was successfully delivered, but she did not survive.

1)   When the first responders worked to get the 4 yr. old out of the wreckage (who only had a bruised hip) she told them, 'Don't worry about me, my friend Abby says it's all going to be okay.' (Her family later confirmed this message to Kristi.)

2)   A benefit was held at Joe's Italian Bistro in Anna for Abigail and Bre, her best friend who lived with them at the time, because both girls waited tables at this restaurant. A local mom, who Kristi had never met, sent her a message the following day stating, 'We attendee the benefit dinner last night and while I don't personally know you, I felt I needed to reach out to you and share this: we sat in a booth and our youngest daughter was sitting next to the window. She kept looking out and giggling. I finally asked her what she was so funny and she said 'oh mom, it's my new friend Abby.' When they got home that night, they pulled up a pic of Bre and Abby and asked their daughter to pick out Abby and she immediately pointed out Abby and said 'that's my new best friend Abby!'

3)   Her sister in law sent her a picture of her fit bit and the song it played during her work out, which she did not have in her playlist and it said 'by Abigail.'

4)   The night of the accident, her Mom's cat, who HATES Kristi, came and slept with her.

5)   One morning she woke up and felt as if someone was sitting on her bed. Yep, Abigail.

6)   Kristi's friend called her one morning and said she had a dream about Abigail and she was sitting on Jesus' lap and they were laughing and she was whispering something in his ear and she turned and saw me. She told me to wait, because she wanted me to give you a message, but I woke up before she could tell me what the message was.

I'm sorry. (I told Kristi THAT was the message. That her little girl is happy, sitting on Jesus' lap and laughing with him!)

7)   When they left the cemetery, she saw a man sitting on a bench and told her Mom to turn the car around. Kristi got out and asked if he was ok, if there was anything she could do for him. He looked up and said, 'Who are you'? She explained and he said, 'I've been sitting here for two days with my Mom's ashes because she wanted to be buried by my brother; but, I can't decide if it's the right thing to do. I was just praying to God to give me a sign, and here you are.' Kristi said, 'Well, I just buried my daughter's ashes and I have a shovel, so I can help you bury her.' He said, 'What I really need is a glass of water!' So, they got him a water bottle and later returned with a pillow, blanket, and food for him. He said, 'What I really need is a glass of water!' So, they got him a water bottle and later returned with a pillow, blanket, and food for him.

I told her that HAD TO BE ABBY! I know EXACTLY how it feels leaving that cemetery after burying Pierce; and there's NO WAY I would have stopped, to talk to a stranger sitting there upon leaving. It was Abby who led her to do that. Kristi, at one point said, 'The night before, as we ate dinner, we always hold hands and pray. Bre yanked her hand away saying she didn't want to be a part of this circle. Kristi said Bre had been questioning her faith and she was worried she was about to go down a bad path and might take Abby with her.

I told her no way; not the Abby she described to me! She would be the steady in her storm and fight to keep her on track. Kristi said, 'Maybe that's it. Maybe that's the reason this happened. When they died in the wreck, Abby grabbed her hand and said 'let's go' and took her up to Heaven with her; thus, saving her from what was about to go wrong in her life and proving to her God, Jesus, and Heaven are real. And, in this process, I've finally gotten friends, like you.'

We shared stories, of Abigail, her Grandfather, her best friend, our kid's similar lives, how our lives run on a similar plane, etc. The similarities, the NUMBERS connection, how we all probably previously bumped into one another.

While saddened by the circumstances, I'm am now blessed with two new wonderful life-long friends! Most of all....I am thankful.

I was SO hesitant upon reaching out to them because, when you lose a child to suicide; often, parents who have lost a child by other means, are angry and resentful towards you; because, their child DID NOT CHOSE TO DIE – YOURS DID! Which of course, is ridiculous; my child died of a disease, depression, no different than cancer; yet, they do not view it this way. (Thankfully, she did not judge and was kind and understanding in Pierce's situation.) We forge on, knowing in our hearts, the truth; thus, my advocacy, to bring suicide and depression to the fore-front to change the image of it and the stigma attached to it.

Bryant (lung recipient) came to Dallas for a check- up and stayed with Tim and I Wednesday night before I left the next day for Chicago. He also stayed Thursday night with Tim. We went to dinner and came back and Tim showed him our new house plans.

On the 13th of July, I flew to Chicago to see my half bio-bro and got to meet my 2 nephews – finally! Tim was supposed to go; but couldn't, because of the house being listed and needing to be here for showings.

On my flight there, I met this wonderful lady who was headed to Chicago for a family reunion and a tug boat caption from New Orleans. She asked me how many kids I had, so the story came out. I had a copy of the book with me, so I gave it to her and told her to read the first ten pages. She did, stopped, wiped her eyes and said, 'Oh lord, you are a strong woman.'

I told them they were going to be Internet famous,
but I don't think they believed me!

When they picked me up at the airport, Luke was wearing P's original lacrosse jersey I have him for Christmas. I brought the boys gifts: model cars that were Pierce's, his first hot wheel, the California flag he got when he went to California with Daddy David and Corn-ho-li-o. They were out-of-their-minds excited over the flag because they went on a fabulous trip there a few years ago. I also brought Luke's birthday present with me, a duplicate of Pierce's cross necklace. He was so proud of it. He would ask if it was ok for him to sleep in it, shower in it, play basketball with it on, etc.

On the ride home from our day in the city, Connor asked me, 'Aunt Bobbi, why do you hate our dad so much?' (this is because Josh and I constantly pick on each other.) My reply was 'well what is there NOT to hate?' Bless his heart, it's hard for a sweetie to understand our sarcasm!

I sat at the kitchen table and Luke came and sat across from me. He looked at me and said, "I wish I had gotten to meet Pierce." I told him 'me too, 'cuz y'all are so much alike!' He asked why, if I've known about them for over 8 years, did I never contact them? And why, when I was in Chicago 6 years ago and knew about them, why didn't I contact them then?

I explained it was because when I first contacted Uncle Danny, it was to get info, medical info, and maybe a photo of Jan, to see where my looks came from, and that I have a great family, great parents; so, I'm not looking for a family, just info. I promised it was not my intent to cause harm or to disrupt lives. I kept my word for 8 years; but, after Pierce's death, that all changed. I felt Josh had a right to know about me, especially since he grew up thinking he was an only child.

I asked him if he had any questions about Pierce and what happened (he knows he committed suicide because he saw the cover of my book, but doesn't know why or any details.) He just sat there. So, I started talking; explaining that he died from a disease, depression; and, we got him help and thought he was getting better, but, he just couldn't get past it. So, he snuck-out in the middle of the night, drove to her house and did it there. I told him all about their toxic relationship, how she used him, toyed with his feelings and emotions, and how Pierce had savior complex, and just wanted to save her from her pathetic life. I told him if he EVER had a girlfriend treat him badly, to break it off and run the other way as fast as he can! He had tears in his eyes as I explained it all.

Luke was bugging Josh about his allowance and how he hasn't been paid it for 3 weeks now, so I stepped in and acted on Luke's behalf as his attorney and drafted this contract for him to enter into with Josh.

July 13, 2017

I, Josh 'half-bio-bro bratty rat' Wheaton will from now on; agree, to adhere, to the fore-set agreement - that will be signed in blood.

If I, (as for mentioned & now referred to as 'I') do not pay Luke J. Wheaton on every Friday by 5:00 p.m. CST, I will pay a 50% intrest, EVERY week, per week, that such allowence payment is not made.

I embark on this agreement, on today, Thursday, July 13, 2017, with Luke J. Wheaton and do bolemly swear to agree to all set terms of this contract as witnessed by Bobbi Danice Morgan Gilbert.

NO WAY
Josh 'Loser' Wheaton

Luke J. Wheaton

date
11:59

July 13 2017
date
11:59

On the first leg of my flight home, I sat between two guys in their mid-forties to fifties. I finally struck up a conversation with one of them and asked where he was from, why he was flying, etc. Since Pierce's passing, I have come to learn, everyone you meet, every encounter, is for a reason.

He finally asked me how many kids I had, and thus; the reason for our connection. When I told him the story, he shared their good friends just lost their 24- year old son to suicide 6 months ago and how badly the mom is struggling. He asked me when will she get better. I told him probably about the 8-month mark, but then she'll slip back.

'There's a bottle, on the dresser by your ring,
and it's empty, so right now I don't feel a thing.
I'll be hurtin', when I wake up on the floor, but I'll be over it by noon.
That's the difference, between whiskey and you.
One's the devil. One keeps driving me insane.
At times I wonder, if they ain't both the same.
One's a liar, that helps hide me from my pain.
One's a long, gone bed of truth.
That's the difference, between whiskey and you.'
'Whiskey and You' – Chris Stapleton

I heard Luke get up the next morning and run back upstairs laughing! Josh couldn't find his knives or coffee pot! They'll be finding stuff for days!

Anniversary dates and birthdays are the hardest. I told him that's why I adopted the philosophy of 'one step forward, two steps back.' I also said, 'as a friend, run to them, not from them' explaining how many friends we've lost since Pierce's passing. I gave him my card and told him to get the book for her to read, that it will help her.

On the last leg of the flight, I sat next to these two lovely newlyweds, Helen and Elray, who is a WWII vet. We're having dinner with them in September when they return from summering in the mountains. We shared our stories and they are now members of #TeamPierce!

'I've seen my share of broken hallos,
folded wings that used to fly.'
'Broken Hallos' - Chris Stapleton

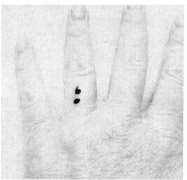

I got this in honor of my new book!

Things people with Social Anxiety do

secrets-obsessions-lies:

survivide:

- go to the bathroom to escape
- feel very uncomfortable without a phone or some other crutch
- dwell on a small awkward moment for much longer than necessary
- never go to any social event without a person that makes you feel comfortable
- follow said person way too much
- worry about the person beginning to find you obnoxious
- faking an illness to get out of a social event
- Don't buy something necessary because the cashier is intimidating.

WOW

One day when Tim and I were getting the house ready for a showing, Pierce told Tim, 'Heck yeah, I'm gonna haunt the new owners, if they don't love it here like we did!' So my boy!

Morgan went on her mission trip to Belize and it was the lifetime experience we wanted it to be for her! She posted this picture with the following statement:
My heart has been forever changed by the children of Belize, and the sweet souls I worked with on this trip. If there is one thing I could take away from this trip, it would be to give, whether it be your time, money or knowledge. No one ever became poor from giving.

On July 20th, news broke that Chester Bennington, lead singer for Linkin Park committed suicide the night before. (YIKES – NUMBERS – same day as Pierce!) This absolutely breaks my heart! We met him when we were on our way to NYC for spring break. We arrived early and it wasn't crowded, as it was so early in the morning. So once we found our gate, we walked to the closest restaurant for breakfast.

We got our food and sat at our table. Pierce was seated across from me and looked up and loudly whispered, "Oh my God! Mom! Look who's behind you at the next table!" I turned around (and of course, he overheard the loud whisper & smiled at me).
I looked back at Pierce and said, "Who is he?"
P: Oh my God Mom!!! You don't know? It's Chester from Linkin Park!
Me: Oh, okay, I see why you're so excited.

look at this precious child

M's speech about nutrition and health

It's a wrap Belize!

At this point, he approached our table and asked if Pierce would like an autograph. Well, we didn't have anything for him to sign, so he asked Pierce if he could sign his shirt. Now, if you know Pierce, he was VERY PARTICULAR about his cloths, so I was shocked when P agreed to him signing it. He went to his wife, got a sharpie and signed it and then took a pic with the kids. Pierce asked him where he was headed to. He said back home to California. They just flew in from Belize, their last stop on their tour.

After we left and got to our gate, I explained to Pierce how incredibly nice he was to do that; because, usually most celebrities do not want to be bothered while traveling; thus, the reason for a body guard.

Tim went into town Friday to do pay roll for our guys. When driving in, the radio station suddenly switched (he didn't do it) and a Linkin Park song came on. Then Chester talked to him, saying, 'You raised a great boy and he's been really helpful and comforting to me up here." Pierce then chimed in and said, "Dad, while he loves it up here, he's really sad and having a hard time. He regrets what he did and that he caused so much hurt to his wife and kids; so, I'm helping him through it."

Then God talked to him about 'the numbers thing' after death, what it means. He said it's the way of connecting us to people who we've known or come into contact with over the course of our lives or past lives. I have now adopted the motto of 'they've crossed over' instead of 'they died'. Our loved ones are not dead; they are simply, on the other side. Always open yourself up, look for signs, they are there, I promise.

Upon my return, I went into town to pick up our desk top Mac computer (the one Pierce begged for continuously until he got it for Christmas, so the joke in our house is 'Mac, Mac, Mac, get a Mac!)

I had Rodi working on it to move the data over to a USB so none of the images or videos Pierce had on there would be lost and then to clear it so none of our personal stuff remain; since, I'm giving it to LaKeshia and her girls. When I arrived, he said, 'I'm up to April 23rd, but had to stop there because I got busy. I'M SO ANGRY AT THAT GIRL! And, for me, knowing you personally, it's different for me reading it than others; because, I actually feel as if I'm walking with you, seeing it through your eyes! And, you've made me think, seriously consider, of becoming an organ donor.'
First, it saved LaKeshia from taking her own life; my friend Laurie signed up to be a donor, and now it's working to get people to register to be donors.
MY MISSION IS ACCOMPLISHED!

LaKeshia had a rough week mid-July. She shared with me that she lost her son after her ex beat her so badly one night. He was too small to survive and this particular day would have been his birthday. Krist, Abagail's mom, is of course, still struggling with it all being too soon. She actually had a doctor say to her, 'Accidents happen all the time, it's time to get over it!' OMG!!!! What the hell is wrong with people. So, doc, when you lose a child, we'll be sure to visit you at the 1 month mark and tell you to get over it! So, I decided I would surprise them and kidnap them and take them to see the movie 'Girls Trip' at IPic.

we call this our reverse oreo photo

It was a great distraction and we had a wonderful time, laughing and sharing our stories. So, now we refer to ourselves as the grieving mama club.

At the end of the month, two teens, who follow my page shared their stories of depression and attempts. I'm SO proud of them for sharing! If more would share, others would know they are not alone in their feelings and emotions! Here are their stories: Krisie:

I want to help people who go through suicidal thoughts and who's been through depression. I want you all to know your not alone, so I'm gonna tell you my story and feel free to share your thoughts with me below. When I was 9 my dad past away. it never hit me that he was really gone until one night, sleeping in my grandparents guest room I woke up crying for my dad. I couldn't breathe it was like losing a part of me.. when I was 15 I moved to Denison thinking that I had it all. A boyfriend who I thought loved me for 9 whole months and a lot of friends. until high school came along I lost my first love because he cheated and disrespected my privacy. Then next, all my friends that I thought was real, was fake. I was so alone and hurt and I never thought of doing drugs until I found out my first love sent my nudes to the school. Everyone calling me a hoe and some people even told me I should die. I never felt so alone in my life. I went home grab a bottle of sleeping pills and put it all down my throat. I close my eyes for the pain to go away .. lucky for me I woke up in the hospital with my grandparents. they took me home after .. I sat on my bed thinking no one cares about me also no one needs me.

I started to cut to take the pain off my mind. I started to take drugs and drink alot with people that didn't care about me or my health. I did the most dangerous and unbelievable mistakes I wish I could take back to this day.. I went to the mental hospital cause my family thought it was safe for me there .

When I got out it was the same. Everyone at my school telling me I ain't shit, that no cares about me. but I have family that loves me and I never wanna put them through pain because of my action. This world is cruel. It takes people away from us, it bullies you, it judge you, it's selfish and it hurts you. all those people that cry at night just know your not alone someone loves you. Sometimes it feels you can't push through life but you can. We can all make it through anything we set our mind to. It will take time but take it day by day. God has you and i. Trust in him.

Chelsea's:
I didnt want to talk about this but i guess its good to and im trying to open peoples eyes when it comes to suicide to so it was summer time i was 17teen i lived in a trailer park i stayed drunk most of the time and made dumb choices but idc i was depressed then i got to the point where i was like none of these people care about me and my family doesn't even talk to me so thats when i begin tryin to kill myself the first three times my sister saved me the last time i ate like 30 blood pressure pills and seizure pills mixed together with vodka my sister and her bbdaddy went to see twilight that day and i was supposed to be watchin my niece but i couldnt and since i didnt pick up my phone they came back i was fadin in and out i was dying i got to the hospital the doctor said someone must have been watching over me the girl in the nxt room died tho and her mother talked to me and i got the chance to live so im gonna make the most of it so yall do the same dont worry about people that arent worried about you be around people who care about you and love you.

Pierce's friends, after his passing:

Wesley:
"At first it was hard. I went to his grave a lot, usually every day, for hours. I would always listen to his songs, especially 'Ballad of a Southern Man' by Whiskey Myers a lot, it was hard. He was more like a brother to me, not just a friend. I see things at work every day, that I think, Bobby would get this. He and my boss would so get it & so get along. They would have gotten along so much better than he and I do.

He taught me that no matter if you have a million dollars or one dollar, it didn't matter. The first time he came over to my house, hell, my shack of a trailer, he just walked right on in, flopped on the couch and made himself at home; no judgment. He taught me, no matter where you are standing, don't judge; cuz, look at him, his life, his upbringing. None of that mattered to him. He treated everyone the same.

So after Bobby, he was my best friend, he was Clay's best friend, and then we both realized, we have each other left. So now, I attach deeply to friendships as in the past, I didn't get attached – it wasn't until Bobby I got deeply attached to someone.

I miss him and still think about him every day. He made me a better person – to make me want to be a better person. I like the idea of the stones at the grave, that's cool!"

Wes is doing really good now. He has a steady job, has stopped drinking, joined the Mason Lodge, and rented a small one-bedroom house in town. His brother is now living with him. He invited us over to show us his place and it was spotless! We're so proud of him!

Karli:

She started college at UNT and after her first semester, moved to England and is attending University there. She will now graduate college at 19 years old. She met a fellow psychology major and they are now dating. She shared that her 2nd boyfriend was suicidal, and she couldn't handle it. When she started dating this guy, one night they were discussing mental health issues and he was about to refer to suicide and she stopped him and said, 'No, don't you say it, don't go there!' She feels as if the 3rd guy she dated was or has been suicidal, then it makes her the common denominator in the equation. Which, is ridiculous, because so many have that in their history.

Race:

When I took Race his graduation gift, it was so sweet. He was happier to see me than to receive his gift! He is attending college in Southern Arkansas and is planning on pursuing a degree in medicine. Last summer, he and his mom, Michelle, went on a mission trip and he was able to participate in an O.R. Race shared with me how his life has dramatically changed since losing Pierce.

He said he now views the world differently; because, his parents really sheltered him from a lot of the ugliness in this world. He feels like Pierce was so aware of it because of his intelligence and always reading and researching things; thus, maybe that was part of all this, him not wanting to live in a world like this. He says he often thinks back on all of he and Pierce's plans for their lives and because of that, he often thinks, what would Pierce do? He feels compelled to be successful for the both of them. He shared the copy of his book with his boss at school. She too, lost a friend to suicide, and after reading it, Race said it really helped her to get answers to questions she's always had and to know that her friend is now okay. He feels my book(s) are very helpful to people by it showing we survived and we're okay.

I know he will be successful in his life, both professionally and personally and am so thankful Pierce had him as one of his best friends!

Clay:
Clay graduated in 2017 and is completing his college courses at Grayson County Community College in welding. Both he and Wesley have joined the Mason Lodge and are continuing to strive and improve their lives. They have become good friends since Pierce's passing and I'm so glad they have each other. His mom told me he has his copy of the book in his room and no one is allowed to move it or touch it.

Darren:
He just completed his first year of college in Arizona and is doing great. He has a wonderful girlfriend and enjoys college life! His Dad was promoted; thus, he was relocated to California. His mom and sister will remain in Allen until she graduates next year.

They shipped his mustang to California and Lisa couldn't decide if his duplicate of P's cross necklace, which hangs from the rear view mirror, should stay in it or if she should keep it with her.

She tried to reach me; but I was unavailable, so she decided to keep it in the car. She knew when the car hauler left, she made the right decision. I told her yes, she did, because P went to Cali once and would love to go back again!

Kenzie:
(She's the one that left the four-page note at Pierce's grave.)
I am SO happy to say that yes, she kept her promise to Pierce! Her promise was, 'now that you're in Heaven and can constantly see me, I promise to stay clean and sober because I told you I never wanted you to see me this way.' She now has a toddler, but has struggled with post-partum depression; but, is getting help for it. I am so proud of her and feel she has a bright future ahead of her!

Cole:
Cole really struggled the first year and a half after Pierce's passing. He became severely depressed and was taking medication for it that was helping; but, the doctor, for some unknown reason, changed the prescription, and he plummeted into depression again. Thankfully, he got help and is doing well. Cole graduated in 2017 and is attending the University of Dallas and playing lacrosse for their team. He is planning on majoring in business and will obtain his MBA. We know the future is bright for him and can't wait to see what it has in store for him!

Dear Gilbert Family,

First off, I am honored that yall chose me for the scholorship and I really am thankful for it. Yall have been like second parents to me and I love you all! Thank you so much for joining me in my graduation celebration. I need to come up and hunt with Timbo sometime!!

Love,
Corn-holio

The Recipients:

David Ray (heart):
He still works for Wal-Mart and is still driving the Mustang! We finally paid it off and sent him the title; but, he knows if he ever gets a different car, we get it back. He is now dating someone and we're so thrilled for him and his happiness. At his last yearly check-up, the doctor told him his heart is perfect and should last him a lifetime!

Alicia a.k.a KP (kidney/pancreas):
Brad and Alicia got married! They have known each other since high school, so she finally got her 'happily ever after!' We're so happy for the both of them! Unfortunately, she was in a wreck the spring of 2017 and fractured her ankle. She thought it was healed, but it's not. She started having issues again and went to a specialist. They x-rayed it and it's now fractured in two places and her foot is fractured in three places. It's due to a combination of things: first, being a diabetic since she was 14 and the anti-rejection drugs are hard on bones as well. We're praying the doctors can find a way to help her and ease her pain!

Bryant (lungs):
He started barber school in the fall of 2016 in Lubbock and is also working at a liquor store; which, he say 'every time I work the drive thru, I always make $22.'
In 2017, he started dating someone, she moved in with him and for him, it was finally love. Upon returning from work one day, 3 months into it; she had packed all her things and left, with no explanation, rhyme or reason.

He became depressed and contemplated suicide. Thankfully, he battled back and is doing better. He told me he now fully understands what Pierce went through. He commented how they are exactly alike. Tim and I have always thought that.

Christina (liver):
In December of 2016, her father lost his life to the same disease she had. She begged him to register to get a transplant; but, he said he had a good full life and didn't want to take a liver from someone young who still had their life ahead of them. Her mom has now moved in with them. She is doing great and loves keeping her precious granddaughter!

We still have not heard from the lady who got his right kidney, even though I sent her a copy of the book. I sent it to her so that she could understand what happened and for her to see that we've met the other recipients and are friends with them.

When the days are cold, and the cards all fold
And the saints we see, are all made of gold.
When your dreams all fail, and the ones we hail,
Are the worst, of all, and the blood's run stale.
I wanna hide the truth, I wanna shelter you,
But with the beast inside, there's nowhere we can hide.
No matter what we bleed, we still are made of greed
This is my kingdom come, this is my kingdom come.
When you feel my heat, look into my eyes,
It's where my demons hide, it's where my demons hide.
Don't get to close, it's dark inside.
It's where my demons hide, it's where my demons hide.
'Demons' – Imagine Dragons

Pierce's poem

You're not here,
and you're still gone;
forever missed,
you are strong.

Lives you touched,
songs you've sung;
ring true today,
forever long.

Your smile is such,
it touches hearts;
deep inside,
never to part.

I miss your love,
each and every day;
and wish you home,
with each prayer I pray...
Forever and always.
-Bobbi Morgan Gilbert

Moments of the night

In the moments of the night,
when every one's asleep;
I can lose my mask,
I can weep.

These are our moments,
these are our times;
when we're alone together,
and the world is mine.

I weep for your loss,
for you I'll always keep;
deep in my heart,
where so many cannot speak.

You'll forever reside there,
for my soul to bear;
a loss that won't be filled,
even when time has breathed its air.

I miss you daily,
almost too much to care.
For the life I live without you,
I'd rather not bear.
- Bobbi Danice Morgan Gilbert

CONCLUSION:

Our lives continue; with each new day, realizing things will never be the same, but, thankfully, we survived it. We are new versions of our previous selves. We make head-way in our grief journey, and we have set backs; thus, my motto, one step forward, two steps back.

The reason for this book, is two fold. 1)To catch everyone up on the lives of his friends, family, and recipients. 2)To complete his story. Yes, suicide awareness/prevention is my advocacy, but I also want Pierce to remembered for the THE WAY HE LIVED; not just, the way he died.

I will continue to:

- advocate for suicide awareness and prevention,
- work with legislators to help bring about reform,
- join groups and boards that lend themselves to my cause.
- my guest speaking engagements and my blog; in hopes of, reaching out to as many people as possible.

I am proud to say, that I am seeing a movement; on my Facebook page, of youth who are not scared to share their stories of depression, self-harm, suicide attempts, etc. THIS IS HUGE!!!!!!! To show others who are suffering, that THEY ARE NOT ALONE!!!!! I AM SO incredibly proud of kids who were brave enough to speak out! If we all, as a community, school district, religious, teachers, counselors, parents, ministers, and civic groups, will speak up about mental health, in particular suicide, we can help end the stigma attached to it; so that our youth know it's okay to ask for help. #0KAYTOSAY

In ALL situations, no matter how dark, there are blessings. The blessings in my life, since April 20, 2015 are:

1) I have become SO MUCH MORE FAITHFUL than I was prior to his passing; praying at every meal, rather in public or private - which is something I never did before.

2) Praying when I wake and when I lay down - thankful for another day. (you may wonder why I'd be thankful for 'another day....another day of hell on earth w/out P. But, I'm thankful for us - we, Tim, Morgan, myself, our family, and our friends, have survived it!!!!!! THAT'S A HUGE BLESSING IN MY BOOK!!!!!!!!!!

3) His passing has led me to reach out to total strangers - who have lost a child, no matter the conditions for losing them - & I feel honored to help them through their journey since I'm 2 yrs down this path.

4) We're one of the few.....the one of the few couples that manage to survive the loss of a child - especially when it's suicide; because spouses often feel guilt and want to place blame on the other. THANKFULLY, God placed Tim in my life...knowing my path and that he'd be the best man to forge me through it and that together, as a team, united, we would SURVIVE!!!!!!

Special thanks to my editors:
Loretta Bruce, M.S.,L.P.C
Shani Grant

For our family & friends:
You're continued love, support, and prayers sustains us.
Thank you for celebrating with us and supporting us through our journey.

Upon completion, please kindly write a review on Amazon.

Blessings, Bobbi